Reflections
I Wish I'd Known

STORIES OF HOPE FOR
WOMEN AND YOUNG WOMEN

PRESENTED BY ERAINA TINNIN

Eraina Tinnin

Reflections
I Wish I'd Known

Stories of Hope for Women and Young Women

Presented By:

Eraina Tinnin

Pearly Gates Publishing, LLC, Houston, Texas

Reflections: I Wish I'd Known

Reflections: I Wish I'd Known
Stories of Hope for Women and Young Women

Copyright © 2018
Eraina Tinnin

All Rights Reserved.
No portion of this publication may be reproduced, stored in any electronic system, or transmitted in any form or by any means (electronic, mechanical, photocopy, recording, or otherwise) without written permission from the publisher. Brief quotations may be used in literary reviews.

Some names and identifying details have been changed to protect the privacy of individuals.

Scripture references marked AMP, KJV, MSG, NIV, NLT, and NKJV are used with permission from Zondervan via Biblegateway.com

ISBN 13: 978-1-947445-01-7
Library of Congress Control Number: 2017962802

For information and bulk ordering, contact:
Pearly Gates Publishing, LLC
Angela Edwards, CEO
P.O. Box 62287
Houston, TX 77205
BestSeller@PearlyGatesPublishing.com

Eraina Tinnin

Special Dedication

This book is dedicated to the **STRONG** women and young women who have survived what they thought they couldn't. It's for those warriors who didn't allow their situation to make them bitter, but make them better.

Reflections: I Wish I'd Known

Acknowledgements

I would be remiss if I didn't give God all the honor, glory, and praise for even the IDEA to compile this book. I had no desire to compile an anthology, but God gave me the idea for the book. For that, I am truly grateful. It enabled me to provide a platform for 15 AMAZING women to share their POWERFUL stories.

Always acknowledging my husband, Corey, and our children, Courtney and Jordan, who support ANY and EVERY thing I do. THANK YOU!

GIVING A SPECIAL THANK YOU to (in no special order) Sima Clark Torian, Nakia P. Evans, Stacey Simmons, Nikki Fisher, Renee Littles, Benita Spinner, Jenyfer Rogers, Lisa Reid Drayton, Tameeka Clark-McClain, Telicia Volter, Toni Freeney, Latia Fisher Ojo, Jekyll, Marcelle Boyd Pettis, and Marchella Blount for choosing MY book to share your story. It was truly a pleasure working with you. You made this project EASY. THANK YOU for meeting all deadlines and being such a joy to work with. THANK YOU for sharing your heart and your soul in this book. I am sure your stories will bless everyone who reads them.

Thanks to Jacques Jones. We were talking one day at work about writing, and he said something about 'reflections'. I said, "That's it! That's the title to my collaboration!" So, the title came from him…and it fits! I appreciate you.

Eraina Tinnin

Thanks to all the ladies in my online ministry, S.I.S. (SistahsInSpirit). We've been rocking for 14 years now. I appreciate each one of you being in my life and for your constant support.

A BIG THANK YOU to all the people who will purchase and read this book. I am sure the stories will encourage, empower, and inspire you.

Introduction

"Bad things happen to good people." Have you heard that saying before? Have bad things happened to you? Have you wondered why? Do you ask God why? At some point in our lives, something bad happens. We may lose a family member, job, or battle an illness. These types of "things" are more common than others. You may even know someone who ALWAYS has something going on or something bad happening to them. They just can't seem to catch a break! This is all too common as well.

In the Bible in Romans 8:28 (NIV), it reads, *"And we know that in all things, God works for the good of those who love Him, who have been called according to His purpose".* This is a very powerful scripture, as it says ALL things work together for the good. ALL things means ALL—EVERYTHING! That means the death of a child, rape, molestation, etc., ALL work together for HIS GOOD. This is a scripture that is quoted often, yet I wonder if people really realize what it's saying. ALL things work for HIS GOOD. In the midst of your trial, tribulation, or challenge, you may not see the good. However, at some point, God will reveal the purpose for your pain. Oftentimes, it is said that you go through something so that later on, you can help someone else. You never know who you may meet who is going through what you already MADE IT through. The purpose of your pain could be to help them so they can have hope that they, TOO, can make it through.

Eraina Tinnin

The 15 amazing stories in this book are powerful. These STRONG women MADE IT through. The stories will have you upset, mad, crying, and in total disbelief. I am sure when they were going through, they didn't see THE GOOD. Some of their good is right here in this book! They are sharing their stories of pain and you will learn how they triumphed. The purpose of their pain is to HELP YOU. They are not VICTIMS; they are VICTORIOUS.

As you read through the pages of this book, I pray you are inspired, empowered, and encouraged by the testimonies shared. I pray the stories give you HOPE if you are currently going through something. They made it…and you can, too!

Reflections: I Wish I'd Known

TABLE OF CONTENTS

Special Dedication vi
Acknowledgements vii
Introduction ix
"He Said He Loved Me" 2
   By Benita Spinner 2
#MyHome 10
   By Jekyll 10
The Optional Child 19
   By Jenyfer Rogers 19
For the Love of Me 28
   By Latia Fisher Ojo 28
From the Inside Out—Know You Are 37
Worth It 37
   By Lisa Reid-Drayton 37
I *AM* Enough 46
   By Marcelle Boyd Pettis 46
Daddy's Girl 55
   By Marchella Blount 55
The Wounds Behind My Mask 63
   By Nakia P. Evans 63
I Took My Power Back Over My Health 71
   By Nikki Fisher 71
Beautifully and Wonderfully Made 80
   By Renee Littles 80

After the Pressing…The Oil Comes 88
  By Sima Clark Torian 88
Abandoned But Not Alone 96
  By Stacey Simmons 96
The Invisible Fire 103
  By Tameeka Clark-McClain 103
Royalty in the Rubble 111
  By Telicia Volter 111
Putting in Work Isn't Enough 118
  By Toni Freeney 118
Words from the Presenter 125
Meet Eraina Tinnin 126

Reflections: I Wish I'd Known

Benita Spinner is a published author and CEO and Co-Founder of the BMS Talent & Entertainment brand. The brand consists of BMSTE Radio Show, #empowerment Queens Rule, BMSTE Apparel, and BMS Talent & Entertainment.

Benita has been recognized by her peers as one the most influential people to know in the DMV area. She was featured in Vital Magazine where she earned the Entrepreneur of the Month Award. She is heavily-involved in several community service projects.

The driving force behind her creating a positive environment is family.

To keep in touch with Benita Spinner visit her website at benitaspinner.com.

Eraina Tinnin

"He Said He Loved Me"
By Benita Spinner

"Oh yes, you shaped me first inside, then out; you formed me in my mother's womb. I thank you, High God—you're breathtaking! Body and soul, I am marvelously made! I worship in adoration—what a creation! You know me inside and out, you know every bone in my body; you know exactly how I was made, bit by bit, how I was sculpted from nothing into something. Like an open book, you watched me grow from conception to birth; all the stages of my life were spread out before you, before I'd even lived one day."

(Psalm 139:13-16, MSG)

Reflections: I Wish I'd Known

<u>My Story</u>

"*But I love you!" "You are the only person for me!" "You are my everything!" "You are beautiful!"* can quickly turn into *"Nobody will want you but me!" "You are ugly!" "No, you can't hang out with your friends. You only need me."*

How does that happen?

My first "boyfriend"—the first person I had sex with—was also the first person to hit me, rape me, destroy my self-confidence, and get me pregnant. My **first** experiences have been defining moments throughout my whole life.

I wish I could say that being raped by him was the first time I experienced a sexual assault, but it wasn't. However, it was the first time I was actually ***raped***.

As a child, I was depressed. "Back then", it wasn't acknowledged in that way. It was called "defiant", "disrespectful", or "out-of-control". I was angry and hurt. This made it easy for a male to come into my life and make me feel special. I wanted to hold on to that feeling at all costs. Through the verbal and physical abuse, I was willing to stay and take it…because he "loved" me—and I wanted to be "loved".

At the time, my mother was the enemy (in my eyes). She was trying to keep me from the only person who loved me. She found all his faults and could not see why I loved him so much. In hindsight, she was right. My mother had no idea what I was going through, but she knew he was not right. I fought her tooth and nail to prove she was wrong. As a teenager, you feel like you are invincible and that you can handle anything that comes your way. There is a consequence to that feeling of being invincible.

At the time, I was living in a world of chaos at home with my mother (who was doing her job as a parent), at school (with a bunch of kids I had very little in common with), and trying to maintain peace in an EXTREMELY dysfunctional relationship. All of these things occurred at the age of 16. They are a lot for an adult, let alone a 16-year-old child who felt like she had all the answers.

The first time my boyfriend slapped me, he told me, *"You better not tell your mother, either. I want her to like me."* So, he would always ensure he hit me in areas she would never see. He had a craving for acceptance from her. I now know that was because of his own insecurities. The acceptance he craved from her I knew he would never get. The best he would get from her was tolerance.

The day I realized I had to figure out how to get out the relationship was the day he put a gun to my head and told me I better not ever leave him. At that point, a light bulb finally went off and I thought, **"This is too much!"** However, I was still unable to tell my mother what was going on in my world. Instead, I stayed angry and lashed out at her.

Reflections: I Wish I'd Known

I did not realize the hell I would endure trying to get out of that relationship. I had yet to tell my mother what was going on with the relationship. I treated my biggest advocate like the enemy because she was making it so difficult for me to be in that relationship. She asked so many questions, gave me curfews, made him come to the door to pick me up, and did not allow me to be alone with him. She treated me like a child!

News Flash: *I WAS A CHILD!*

The day I told him I wanted to break up was the day I began to live in fear. He would show up at my school out of nowhere. I had to go in late or leave early so he would not know whether or not I was even in school that day.

I remember one day, he found out I was over a friend's house. He came over there and chased me down with his car, then he jumped out and started choking me. My friends were yelling and trying to pull him off of me. He finally stopped. You guessed correctly if you thought, "Then she got in the car and left with him". He drove me home and told me, *"This is where you belong if I am not with you. Get out of my car"*.

At that point, things got worse because my friends now knew what was going on—which added an additional layer of pressure to the situation.

After that public display of abuse, I became completely over it and told him in all finality to leave me alone. Somehow, he got the picture…but only for a few weeks. He came around and knocked on the door. My mom (unaware of what was going on) told me he was there. Reluctantly, I went to the door. He had called the house several times prior to just popping up on my doorstep. I kept hanging up on him. He knew I was not going to make a scene because of my mother.

He apologized and said he wanted to make our relationship work. I told him, *"No. I am over it and think we should go our separate ways"*. He became furious, pushed me into the back of his car, and raped me. I screamed, yelled, and fought—all to no avail. No one helped me. Afterwards, he tried to convince me that it wasn't rape because we were boyfriend and girlfriend and that no one would believe me. I jumped out of his car and ran back into the house. I still didn't say a word to my mother—my advocate and the one who loved me more than life itself. Instead, I blamed her for not stopping something she knew nothing about.

Even though he spent a lot of time trying to tell me he did nothing wrong, he told his friends he raped me. *"That is what she gets for trying to leave me!"* I stood there listening in shock. He kept coming around or finding me at other places. He made my life a living hell!

A few weeks later, he stopped coming around. I was finally at peace. I was having these pains in my stomach and felt so sick. My mother took me to the hospital where the doctor informed us I had a cyst on my ovary…and that I was pregnant. My mother was furious! In her eyes, I messed around and got pregnant. She had no idea the child was conceived due to rape. Yes, it was rape because I said **"NO!"**

My mother was not having it. I was four weeks pregnant and could not have the abortion my mother scheduled until I was a little over six weeks. Instead of me just moving on, I called and told my boyfriend. He came over and told me I was dumb for getting pregnant because now, my mother will hate him. He jumped up and kicked me in my stomach with both feet and jumped into his car, never to be seen again.

This from a man who "loved" me! This from a man who told me I was the only person for him! This from a man who said I was his EVERYTHING!

Eraina Tinnin

I Wish I'd Known

My mother was my advocate; not my enemy. I wish I'd known that real love was between my mother and I. Loving yourself is the most important gift you can give yourself.

Words of Inspiration

We have a choice to believe what we want to feel or hear. Make sure you have a clear understanding of the truth. Lies, hurt, and pain can come in all types of forms and appear real. My choices were not smart because I believed an illusion of truth. He told me he loved me. I believed it. I believed that the love he offered was pure and the love my mother offered was stopping me from achieving true happiness.

Ensure you have a great understanding of your choices, as they affect your past, present, and future. I no longer beat myself up for my choices; nor do I blame my mother. My choices were mine. I have had many struggles, but am now a walking testimony that you can get through with prayer and by ensuring you have positive people in your corner.

Reflections: I Wish I'd Known

Jekyll is an up-and-coming novelist. Raised in New Castle, Delaware; this writer makes a living as a Registered Nurse. She attended both University of Delaware and Helene Fuld School of Nursing.

An active member of the motorcycle community, this lady is an Administrator of a biker group with over 17,000 members. The group focuses on safe riding, community, and fellowship.

Trying her hand at acting, Jekyll is hopeful of landing that breakthrough role. She continues to write, enjoys cooking, working out, and, of course, catching wind on her bike while she waits.

Eraina Tinnin

#MyHome
By Jekyll

"But we also glory in our sufferings, because we know that suffering produces perseverance; perseverance, character; and character, hope."

(Romans 5:3-4, NIV)

My Story

I had always been the proverbial "Black Sheep" of the family. It became obvious when I was 10 years old. I was standing outside of the bathroom door in my grandmother's house. I remember knocking on the door, my mother opening it and then yelling, *"It's a shame to say that I hate my own child…**but I hate you!**"* That's the moment I realized: I didn't fit in my family.

Every day, my mother's words began to ring louder. I began to spend as little time as possible at 'home'. By the time I was 13, I would sneak off regularly. Many nights, I would sneak out my bedroom window and run off to the local hangout. I would climb out of the window onto the roof with my sister. We'd then jump the fence and climb down to the ground. Eventually, we moved out of our grandmother's house and into a one-story house—which made our nightly adventures even easier.

Shortly after moving, I met 'Greg'—an up-and-coming basketball star in the neighborhood. I'm not sure if I was more interested in him or he in me. All I knew was that someone I liked, liked me! Until that point, I had lived in the shadows of my sisters. They were beautiful and I was (according to my mom) "bald-headed and big-eyed". Greg and I quickly moved to an intimate relationship. In my head, in order to keep Greg's attention, I had to have sex with him.

I loved kids and had a great relationship with my two-year-old niece. Wherever I was, she was not far behind. Even with this, I never wanted to have kids of my own. I never wanted any child to feel the way I did. Every child deserves to feel loved.

Armed with my determination to not get pregnant coupled with my resolve to stay with the boy who wanted me, I decided to sleep with Greg. I would wait exactly two weeks after my period so that it was "out of my system", and then I would sleep with him. Being the tomboy that I was, my only sex talk was, *"If you have sex when you start your period, you will get pregnant"*.

Well, I missed one period…and then another. I knew I was pregnant. One day, I decided that this wasn't the life I wanted. I went into the bathroom, opened the medicine cabinet, and grabbed the first thing I found. I swallowed a handful of pills. I remember walking into the kitchen and vomiting. My mom began yelling, **"YOU'RE PREGNANT!"** I ran back to the bathroom, with my dad close behind. I grabbed the bottle of pills again and took another handful. My father slapped both me and the bottle out of my hand. In the chaos, I was able to tell my mother I did not want to have a baby. Her response was, *"What kind of person would kill their baby? Your sister never wanted to kill her baby!"*

In my head, all I could hear were her echoes of,

"I hate you…I hate you…I hate you…"

When I was 15, our daughter was born. Greg never became the basketball star we once thought he would, so he turned to selling drugs. Our relationship ended within a year. My mother helped take care of my daughter until I finished high school and my first year of college.

During my senior year of high school, I met my high school sweetheart and his mother, Mrs. Brown. Mrs. Brown gave me a new perspective of what family looked like. She took me in and motivated and nurtured me as her own child. The two of them made me begin to feel like maybe there was something different out there for me. I was with her son until my sophomore year of college, but she remained a very important part of me and my daughter's lives until the day she died some years later.

In 1989, I met the man I would marry. I was a college sophomore and he was months away from graduation. I never understood it, but he worshipped the ground I walked on. He and I moved in together, and I was finally away from "that house". Shortly after, my mother died at the age of 38 from breast cancer.

My husband made me believe in fairytales. Two years into our marriage, I became pregnant with twins. After losing two babies, I couldn't believe that God had blessed me with two babies at once! I became a stay-at-home mom and even home-schooled my kids for a while. My family had become my life. I finally did something that would have made my mother proud.

Fifteen years into my marriage, the fairytale ended. Infidelity made me realize that my life was a lie. The happy home in which I lived was a façade. Not only was I yearning for something more, so was he. I had failed at this, too. As I struggled to keep my family intact, I could hear my mother's voice: "I hate you…"

I remained in the marriage for almost another five years. We went on with business as usual, even having a vow-renewal ceremony in Las Vegas. One day, I woke up and knew it was time to call it quits. For months, I would wake up early before the kids, sit at the top of the steps staring out the huge foyer window, and just cry. My spirit was crying for something else—and had been for years. The cries were so loud, I could no longer ignore them.

I was sitting at my cousin's husband's funeral surrounded by people I didn't know, watching them cry for the loss of this man. My cries were different. I cried because I worried what my cousin's life would become. I cried because of how much life he would miss. I cried because one day, that would be me. I cried because I wanted to feel loved the way she clearly loved him. I cried because I wanted my life to mean something.

That day, I left my husband.

Losing my family was devastating, yet I knew that in order to save ME, I had to let go. The next few years were hell. My kids hated me for leaving, and he constantly tried to get me to come back. This was one of the most difficult times in my life. Now, not only did I hear my mother's *"I hate you…"*, I could also hear my kids screaming, **"I HATE YOU!"**

Reflections: I Wish I'd Known

I had sunk so deep into a dark place that I became reckless in both my associations and behavior. I needed to pull myself up out of there or I would never recover. I had to find the silver lining. I asked myself, *"What was one thing I always wanted to do but couldn't because I was married?"* My answer was, **"Ride a motorcycle."** Within a week after that revelation, I purchased a motorcycle and was riding!

My husband had given me a life of luxury: a big, beautiful home, cars, vacations…anything that money could buy. Meanwhile, I had lost myself. I had no idea who I was or what I wanted anymore. I spent the next few years rediscovering myself on my motorcycle, riding up and down the East coast. I quickly realized: This is who I am! I am a biker! I had never felt freer and at home than when I was on my bike and in the biker community. This is the one place I fit in. I didn't have to pretend. I could just be me!

The people and the bonds I formed became my family. I became very active in the biker community. I am an advocate for female bikers. In addition, I am an Administrator for a motorcycle group of over 17,000 members that promotes education and safe riding. We also emphasize brotherhood and sisterly-love.

This is what my spirit was screaming for. My passion led me to my purpose. My motorcycle has been the catalyst to many opportunities and has led me to places I would have never imagined for myself, including an acting career. I have found my home in people who love me. I tell my kids I love them every opportunity I get. I have a granddaughter who is my latest joy—and my ex-husband is still one of my best friends…and I haven't heard my mother's 'voice' in years.

I Wish I'd Known

To be truly happy, you must live authentically. You don't have to fit into anyone else's idea of who you should "be". Not fitting in is what made me special.

Words of Inspiration

God's love is the greatest love of all. In His eyes, you will always fit in.

Eraina Tinnin

Jenyfer Rogers is an entrepreneur who combines her love for the entrepreneurial and small business industry with her passion for education. She is an active Realtor and also serves as a Financial Representative.

Jenyfer's mission is to empower people to attain personal financial success. She is an active Speaker on subject such as real estate, credit, and finances. She is also the Founder of The E.Y.E. Network, which is now in its second year.

She is a mother of six and lover of all things food. She enjoys spending time with family and friends, as well as traveling.

Reflections: I Wish I'd Known

The Optional Child
By Jenyfer Rogers

"Concerning this thing I pleaded with the Lord three times that it might depart from me. And He said to me, "My grace is sufficient for you, for My strength is made perfect in weakness." Therefore, most gladly I will rather boast in my infirmities, that the power of Christ may rest upon me. Therefore, I take pleasure in infirmities, in reproaches, in needs, in persecutions, in distresses, for Christ's sake. For when I am weak, then I am strong."

(2 Corinthians 12:8-10, NKJV)

Eraina Tinnin

<u>My Story</u>

For the life of me, I can't remember when I made up my mind to have a baby. All I knew was that they were cute and they seemed to love their mom very much…and I wanted one. I wanted one so badly that when a girl in middle school got pregnant, I started to dream about my own baby. I even had a picture of one of my little cousins and would tell my peers that she was my baby! I bet you are thinking, "Fast behind little girl". I really wasn't, though. I was interested in the act of getting the baby or the boy needed to get the baby. My ultimate goal was to have a baby. I bet you are wondering, "Why? Why would a baby want to have a baby?"

Let me help you understand…

Growing up, I remember watching a television series called "Touched by an Angel". I would cry and wonder, *"Where is my angel?"* I couldn't understand what it was about me. Why was I unloved and unwanted? As an adult, I wondered the exact same thing. Ever since I was a little girl—as far back as I can remember—people would look at me with pity. A few times, I ran into some of my mom's old girlfriends, and they would hug on me and say how they were glad I was okay. It looked like I turned out good!

"I used to worry about you", they would say.
"It always bothered me the way your mother would talk to and treat you", they would say.

Reflections: I Wish I'd Known

I would just smile, shake my head, and tell them I was doing okay. I would always walk away wondering: If they truly felt like that, why didn't they ever say anything? Why didn't they intervene? I guess like children, it was best to be seen and not heard...or maybe they were just simply minding their own business.

I grew up with my maternal grandmother. My mother was a teenage mom who, from her side, sounds like one of those generational history situations. I was told that I was with my grandmother since I was two years old. My brother's dad said that he couldn't bear to sit and watch the way my mom treated and abused me. So, he packed up all my stuff and dropped me off to live with my granny.

Now, my ma says that I lied and told the police she hit me with a belt. I don't know if the police asked a two-year-old what happened (because I don't remember). My mom said she told the police and the judge to "...take this lil 'B' and give her to the big 'B'". That's kind of how the downward battle began.

Would you believe she ***still*** tells the story the exact same way, void of feeling or remorse?

I remember sitting with my head down and crying when I was in the 2nd or 3rd grade. I had this picture of my two brothers that I would carry around and just look at it. My mental breakdowns began at an early age. When I was in 3rd grade, my mom showed up at my school and told the principal something. I don't know what she said, but it must have been good because he pulled me out of class to let me see her. It was real emotional. She hugged me and told me how much she loved me and that I would be coming home with her real soon. We ended up going to court and you guessed it: I went home with my mother.

It didn't last very long. It never did. I was back with my grandmother and at a different school the following year. I could never do anything right. It seemed like anything I did when I was with my mom would trigger her. She would pack me up and drop me back off at my grandmother's house. It was like I was an option…I didn't matter.

I remember one Saturday morning, she was asleep. She often slept in late. Since I was the oldest, I made an attempt at making breakfast for my younger brothers. I grabbed the toaster oven out of the kitchen, took it into the living room, and placed it by the front door so I could use the outlet. I was making us toast while we watched cartoons. I was in the 4th grade and didn't know the heat would burn a hole in the carpet. Needless to say, she was beyond furious. She beat me, packed up my clothes, and dropped me off yet again. I was scared of her and loved her so much at the same time. All I wanted was for her to love me back. I wanted her to love me like she loved my brothers.

Scenarios such as these were forever going on. The back and forth was too common. I didn't know any better. Each time she showed up, there were no words to express the feelings I felt for her to "come and get me". In all honesty, it is still kind of like that this very day. I have learned to accept who she is and to enjoy the time with her while I am allowed to be in her life.

Eraina Tinnin

I Wish I'd Known

Remember that baby I so desperately wanted? Well, I got him! That's right: a boy! My 10th grade year in high school, I got pregnant. I didn't care. All I knew was I finally had someone to love me back. I wish I'd known what was needed to be a good parent. I wish I'd known the sacrifices that needed to be made. I wish I'd known the life I would be permanently giving up. I wasn't going off to college. I wasn't going to live in a dorm. I wish I'd known that when I was in my 20s (or even 30s) that I would sit back and look at life and what could have been if I hadn't been a teenage mom. I wish I'd known the importance of REALLY knowing the person I chose to have a baby by. I wish I'd known the health history, characteristics, and personality of my child's father and how those things would play an important role in the behaviors my baby would possess. I was so blind. I was so uninformed. I couldn't see nor understand the way my life would change by having the baby I so desperately wanted. Most importantly, I didn't know that it's not the babies really loving you back; all babies cling to whoever is there to feed and comfort them when they cry. Babies are the same way with everyone. I wish I'd known that I would have to comfort my baby because their dad didn't bother. I wish I'd known that my baby would grow up to FEEL exactly how I did, although I gave and showered him with all the love and attention within me. It somehow wasn't good enough. I wasn't good enough and yet again, I didn't matter. I was an option to the very baby I so desperately wanted to love me. I wish I'd known that one day, my baby would be a child and then a man, doing any and everything to get his father's attention. I wish I'd known that one day, my baby was going to ask, *"Why does everyone else have a dad but me?"* All of these things, I wish I'd known.

If I had known then what I know now, I cannot say 100% that I would have been so adamant about wanting to have a baby. I definitely would not have made the choices and participated in the acts with the same person to create such a beautiful life. Knowing what I know now, I was being selfish. I just assumed that because I would love my baby so much, his father would, too.

Eraina Tinnin

Words of Inspiration

Please know that even though you may feel alone, you are not. God is there. I promise you. It's kind of like the popular Footprint portrait. It is during those times when we feel so broken and forsaken, even scared and alone, when God is carrying you. You are beautifully-made. You can do ALL things through Christ Jesus who strengthens you. Take your time and pray that God anoints you to hear and follow the path He has aligned for you. Even though there was a lot I didn't know, God knew everything before the foundation of the world. You will be okay! You must know and believe that! There are people and places that have been strategically placed to assist you in getting to your destination and providing all you need—right down to this project being put together AND you reading this book! Just let go and let GOD!

Reflections: I Wish I'd Known

Latia Fisher Ojo was born and raised in Baltimore, Maryland. She attended Community College and holds an Associate's Degree in General Studies. She has worked in banking and finance for five years, as well as the industrial field for six years.

Latia is an Author, Poet, and Co-Owner of S&L Mobile Paint Night, LLC. She is also a poetry performer and goes by the name PoemsByTia.

Her passion is love, as she strives her hardest to promote it in every way possible; from her poetry to her business. She has no plans of slowing down anytime soon.

Eraina Tinnin

For the Love of Me
By Latia Fisher Ojo

"To acquire wisdom is to love oneself; people who cherish understanding will prosper."

(Proverbs 19:8, NLT)

Reflections: I Wish I'd Known

My Story

Sometimes, you fear that which you still struggle with in order to know truths. The truth is evident that you have to know love in oneself to truly fully express love to others. I struggled some days to look in the mirror. Some never knew I was bluntly disgusted with the dark-skinned woman who looked back at me.

Since I was a child, I could only remember being bullied and talked about. Even then, I was silent. I will never forget the day someone took my shoes and hid them from me while on the playground at school. My mom had to come to the school. I was so embarrassed, I cried. It was a hurtful feeling, but it was one I will never forget.

The older I grew, the more I continued to struggle. I grew up in a single-parent home with a parent who spent most of her life supporting and providing for her children. She dated often, but those relationships didn't last. She—just like countless other women—wanted and hoped for love. My father was absent, and my mother provided me with the best love she could give. I later built a relationship with my dad.

I grew up pushing others to love and giving love to others the best I could. I would make sure I could always do, always give, and be what I could for everyone else. For a long time, I was in the shadows supporting, encouraging, just being whatever I could to and for other people. Depression slowly crept up on me about a year ago. It was at that moment I realized (after losing a brand-new car, my first apartment, and what I thought would be my sanity): I was left blank and confused because I was being everything to everyone else. I didn't take care of the things that needed to be done for me! When things got rough for me, I didn't ask for help. Instead, I would work two, sometimes three jobs.

At the age of 26, I had given my complete heart and my hard-earned money away. I was left with nothing. Oftentimes, you must go through things to see what they look like on the outside. I was so disgusted with who I was simple because I didn't "know her". I was disgusted because I didn't "love her". I was lost. My friends would tell me all the time, *"Just focus on you and do what you need to do for you."* I didn't listen and found myself much like an empty glass of water: I gave everyone else a sip, and there I was…dehydrated and thirsty. I was void of **ME**.

I had to search deep and figure out what those things were that could make me happy. What were the things that could bring me joy? I found a lot of reassurance in my poetry. I was a woman with words, and my words were my way of no longer being silent. They allowed this new beauty to appear not only within my soul, but also with my appearance. God allowed me to learn who I was through my purpose. He gave me what I needed for me and still allowed me to give to others. The problem was I had to refill my glass and rehydrate myself in order to move forward.

Reflections: I Wish I'd Known

Every day is a process, but some days you have to walk by a mirror and remind yourself that you're the greatest gift. I learned every bit of my strength through my experiences. It pushes me each and every day. We all love to play the 'blame game'. In any situation, one should always evaluate if there is something they could have done differently. False hopes, mixed-emotions, and discomfort all lead to heartbreak. Heartbreak stems from that which we believe to love. When your heart is hurting, you don't immediately think of these things because you're sad; however, imagine discovering your worth once you remove those false hopes. Mixed-emotions and discomfort are no longer. Determination, confidence, and motivation are all my ingredients for self-love.

I was recently talking to a friend about an experience I look back on today and realize how much I hurt myself. I was 17, maybe close to 18, and remember allowing myself to engage in intercourse for the first time with a guy who I had only known for a few months. I wasn't completely ready (and I knew that), but I thought that by allowing it to happen, the guy I thought I loved at the time would be hurt by it. The next day after it happened, I got rid of the guy and blocked his number, never to talk to him again. Guess who was left with the decision she made? I think about that all the time.

Don't do things as if to believe it'll hurt someone else. You are more important than trying to prove something to someone who doesn't know your worth. Not loving yourself will have you so consumed in what the world thinks of you and not what you think of yourself. You must not look for validation from anyone.

I Wish I'd Known

I wish I'd known that loving me was something my parents couldn't teach me. It did not come with a manual, but if I'd known that, I would have started learning at a young age and some of my experiences may not have been as hurtful. I wish there were more programs to help young girls empower and motivate themselves. I see a lot more of them today than when I was younger. I wish I had known how precious my worth was. I wish I had known how precious my mind, body, and spirit are. I wish I had known to believe more in myself and to have invested time in becoming better into myself instead of others. I wish I had known that you can only love a person but so much until it becomes destructive to the heart. I wish I would have known to let a lot of things go to give myself more opportunity to grow. I wish I would have known that you can give as much as you can to someone else, but that will never mean you will get that in return. I wish I would have known not to dwell so much on my mistakes because then, I would have been able to move forward. I wish I would have known loving yourself is an action.

Eraina Tinnin

Words of Inspiration

    Be mindful to feed your soul first. Be mindful that you must 'drink' first. Be mindful that whatever you choose to pour into someone else, you've fully given to yourself first. Be confident in who you are. It's okay to always learn about yourself but never okay to not know who you are. Understand that with knowing and loving who you are, you become knowledgeable. Ask yourself these questions, often if you must: What will bring me true happiness? Am I doing that which will make me happy? Who holds the power; me or my emotions? If your emotions are what you've answered, then you've got some work to do because you must know that you control your emotions. Know that working on yourself is an everyday process. The older you become, the more you experience; the more you grow and learn as a person. The best advice I can give is to learn that love resides inside of you. Learning to love your flaws, your imperfections, as well as your weakness is all a part of who you are. The world will not necessarily create a space for you. You should create your own space and own room in this world. Daily, remind yourself of goals and things you've accomplished—no matter how big or small. Don't ever put yourself down. Be your #1 cheerleader. One of the hardest things is to keep pushing when you feel like you cannot go on. Be your own strength and don't ever be afraid to ask for help. Don't be prideful. There will come a time in your life when you will fall and will need someone. Pay your bills first before deciding to help someone else. Remember that if you have faith in yourself, you will have hope. For that reason alone, you will always be able to love yourself. Be to yourself what you want others to be. Know that you are loved, and don't allow anyone to tell you different.

Always passionate about writing, Lisa M. Reid-Drayton began her love for writing at the early age of five with sweet poems to her mother. That later turned into writing for her yearbook and newspaper staff during her high school and college years. With a B.A. in Broadcast Journalism, Lisa continues to write poetry on a more personal scale and loves to journal.

Currently a Licensed Realtor in the state of Georgia, Lisa states, "Writing always helped save my life!" and looks forward to compiling an Inspirational Daily Devotional and a collection of what she calls "Emotional Love Poems" in the near future.

Reflections: I Wish I'd Known

From the Inside Out—Know You Are Worth It
By Lisa Reid-Drayton

"God is in the midst of her; she shall not be moved; God shall help her, just at the break of dawn."

(Psalm 46:5, NKJV)

Eraina Tinnin

My Story

What do you do when you're told, *"You weren't supposed to be here"*? It literally paralyzed me in my mind. I finally understood why I felt the way I did for so many years. I share my story of a little girl, a teenager, a young woman, and now a middle-aged woman who fought with herself for so many years to know that "Yes: I am worth it!" I struggled for years with issues of low self-esteem and self-worth, always wondering if I was good enough. It is a feeling so many of us battle with, but the joy is finally discovering that yes, YOU ARE GOOD ENOUGH and yes, YOU ARE WORTH IT!

I come from what so many call a "broken home". My parents were going through a divorce after being married six years. At the time, my mom was pregnant with me. I'll never forget the day when I was well into my late 20s during one of my visits home to Charleston, South Carolina. My mom and I were having a conversation that was pretty in-depth, talking about life and some of the challenges that come with it. She opened up and shared how I almost didn't make it into this world. My eyes began to open wide and my heart felt heavy when she said, *"You weren't supposed to be here...I was going to terminate my pregnancy with you."* In complete shock, I asked, **"Mommy, what do you mean?"** She then let me know the stress she faced while going through a separation-turned-divorce with my dad, while having to raise my older sister who was six years old at the time.

It was just too much, especially when she was told, *"I don't care what you do with that baby!"* The doctors advised her to terminate her pregnancy with me because it was just too much. They told her, *"This baby will suffer tremendously healthwise if you carry it full-term"*. At those words, I can only imagine what she must have felt. Not wanting to jeopardize the life or health of her unborn baby, she took the doctors' advice and signed the consent forms to have her pregnancy with me terminated.

I remember looking into my mom's eyes as she continued to share, seeing both sadness and strength all at once.

To myself, I thought, **"Wow! I wasn't supposed to be here? Wow! I wasn't even considered before I had a chance? Wow! Why didn't he want me? Wow! What did I do?"**

I remember mommy saying, *"Lisa, I did sign those termination papers and prepared myself for the procedure"*. She let me know she wrestled with her decision so much that when she went to sleep the night before, a nightmare awakened her. She jumped up and told herself, **"I can't do it! I just can't do it!"** Ironically, it was a nightmare that brought my soon-to-be death to life. I like to always believe—even to this day—that it was the voice of our Almighty Heavenly Father that shook her in her sleep and reminded her, *"You can't do it. You **can't** get rid of that baby!"* Just like that, her mind was changed. I thank God about it!

When you begin to take in the words "not being wanted", it will challenge you and for me, it did. The thing is this: I didn't quite realize just how much until I began to dig deeper. I've seen myself go through so many patterns of self-destruction just to validate my worth, from seeking the constant approval of people to being in unhealthy and damaging relationships—all the while thinking, "I will never be good enough". For a young girl growing up without her dad, it damaged me because I always believed if I wasn't good enough for him to want me, surely I wouldn't be good enough for anyone else. It made me question myself numerous times throughout my life. The behaviors I developed never played in my favor until I realized where my true worth was.

One of the things I desired was to have the approval and love of my dad. I remember so many times trying to have a relationship with him, but it seemed my efforts always failed. A father is truly the first relationship where a girl learns how to be treated by a man. It typically sets the tone for what she should expect from a man. For me, because I didn't get to experience that modeling, I sought it out in other ways. I was a "boy-crazed" little girl and teenager. I think I was the most "girliest" tomboy I knew, but realized it was an effort to get the approval of a male figure. Playing with the boys began to turn into more. After a while, it became what I perceived as "right" (which was far from the truth). I was so desperate to be loved and accepted to be deemed "worthy" that I found myself "falling in love" at a very early age, which resulted in premarital sex. Although my mom (who was and still is very strong-willed and strong minded) raised us the right way in a Christian home and the best way she knew how, it still felt like something was missing.

I remember the "talks", but it's almost like they went in one ear and right out the other. I thought surely, by "giving myself away", it would be the best way I could gain the approval of a man. Unbeknownst to me, boy was I wrong! The more I gave myself away, the less I began to feel about myself. I often heard, *"You're so pretty, you have a beautiful smile, and you're smart, too!"* It just didn't register with me. I didn't believe it for myself because it never came from the person I wanted it from the most. For some reason, I felt like I need to give even more of myself and be more of what the other person wanted, just to have their approval. My outward appearance never reflected what I was truly feeling on the inside, which was often a feeling of emptiness and worthlessness.

High school and college years soon went by and lots of accomplishments were made, but I still found myself with a void. Something was still missing. I even remember when I accepted Christ as my personal Lord and Savior for myself during my freshman year in college, I felt a newfound love, but I don't think I truly understood it. I knew I would misinterpret what I thought was "true love", "true self-worth", and "self-esteem" with things that were completely opposite. Always looked at as "the sweet, nice girl", the pressure to be accepted and please everyone continuously weighed on me. So many times, I would tell people *"Yes"*, when inside, I really wanted to say ***"No!"*** Developing a passive-aggressive behavior, I often wondered how I would break free? How would I know that without the approval of anyone, I would still be deemed "worthy" and still be "loved"? It took years of being in an unhealthy relationship where I accepted so many things I shouldn't have but was too afraid to walk away because I felt like *"This is what I deserve"*, *"This is what it's supposed to be like"*, and *"At least he wants me"*…but still losing so much of myself. It wasn't until I rededicated my life back to Christ after going through a whirlwind of experiences that should have taken me out because of what I had learned to accept, that I slowly began to realize what that "true love" was. That "true love" would help me see my self-worth and raise my low self-esteem.

After going through a near-death health experience almost 10 years ago, and then finding out shortly after that I would never be able to naturally birth a child, it began to weigh on my self-worth and self-esteem once again—but God had a different plan for me. He knew when He shook my mother in her sleep that night to let her know, *"You can't get rid of this child. This child must live and not die because she has destiny. This child has purpose. This child will be loved. This child is worth it!"*, it caused me to look at my life differently. I began to truly look at myself from the inside out and see myself the way God saw me: "Fearfully and wonderfully made in His image" and "a workmanship created for good works". I finally made a decision that regardless of what person—whether parent, spouse, or friend—doesn't want or value you, God does and He will always see you as a beautiful creation full of worth. That alone helped save my life so that I could truly begin to live!

I Wish I'd Known

I wish I'd known that I never had to seek the approval of man, but only of God. Everything we are and everything we do should be unto Him; not unto man. I wish I'd known that I never had to give myself away or settle for less than I truly deserved.

Words of Inspiration

There's someone out there who may feel just like I did: "not worthy" or "not good enough", always trying to please people who truly don't deserve what you have to give. I want to encourage you today and remind you that you are worth it, you are valuable, and you are beautiful from the inside out. You don't have to overcompensate yourself to get the approval of others. God created you in His image. Remind yourself every day what God says about you, not what man says or thinks about you. Some people may tell you, *"Oh, you're too 'this' or you're too 'that'!"* If that's how God created you, embrace it and always walk in your truth. No two people are alike. We are unique in our own right because that's how God created us to be. Always know who you truly are! How do you do that? Read and study God's Word and affirm it over your life daily. Speak life over yourself every day and know you were created for a purpose. More importantly, you must learn to love yourself enough to truly love yourself so that you will know you deserve God's best!

Reflections: I Wish I'd Known

Marcelle Boyd Pettis is a native of North Carolina and has lived in Raleigh most of her life. She has enjoyed a career in school counseling for 21 years. She has a passion for helping young people discover their inner-beauty and talents within.

Marcelle is the product of two educators who dedicated their lives to mentoring and teaching young people. She found greatness in continuing on their paths.

She is a divorced woman who has an amazing 14-year-old son, which is the best part of her. This work is dedicated to him.

Eraina Tinnin

I AM Enough
By Marcelle Boyd Pettis

"Love is patient, love is kind. It does not envy, it does not boast, it is not proud. It does not dishonor others, it is not self-seeking, it is not easily angered, it keeps no record of wrongs. Love does not delight in evil but rejoices with the truth. It always protects, always trusts, always hopes, always perseveres."

(1 Corinthians 13:4-7, NIV)

Reflections: I Wish I'd Known

My Story

As a young college woman, I longed to be liked and loved unconditionally. Who doesn't? Little did I know how hefty of a price that would be. When you give so much of yourself, so freely to so many, and there's no return, you start to ask yourself, *"What's wrong with me? Am I not enough?"*

College is a time to spread your wings, meet new people, and explore a newfound independence. My parents weren't at arms' length every day, so I was charged with making good choices for myself. I thought I was doing a good job until…*I started dating*. Now, I was no ugly girl. In fact, I was kind of cute—*so I thought* and was often told. I had a cute shape and a good head on my shoulders. My parents taught me well and were exceptional providers for my every need. After getting one year of college under my belt, I thought I had life all figured out. *NOT!* I liked having fun and often found myself gravitating to those who shared that desire. I just knew I'd find some likely mates at the many parties I went to…*or so I thought...*

My lack of self-confidence and self-worth came to life while I was high school. I was often bullied because of how I talked, where I lived, how I dressed, or the type of classes I took. The mean words, physical threats, and ultimately, the spit that landed on my face were just enough to make a non-violent chick [try to] turn violent! The mean words were just that—*words!* But that spit wad took on a whole new meaning of defense for me. So, by graduation, I was ready to try life in a different city and environment. I was ready and equipped for a new life....*so I thought.*

Life in the late 80s was much different from the life we now experience: no internet, no cell phones, and of course, no social media. There was more face-to-face communication and interaction. Life was good and very personal. As luck and my poor study habits would have it, I ended up spending five years as an undergraduate student. During my time as a budding, young adult, I learned some very hard lessons. Because of bullying, low self-confidence, lack of maturity, and a trust factor that included everyone, I allowed people to abuse me in more ways than I care to remember. I surely was not immune to physical abuse.

Abuse comes in so many different forms, with physical abuse being the one that most people can "see". The bruises, black eyes, cuts, burns, and other visible scars take time to heal and can leave emotional scars. However, the other forms of abuse—such as emotional, mental, verbal, sexual, spiritual, and financial—aren't as easy to detect but, oftentimes, can take just as long to heal. I endured some of these...along with the physical abuse. A sister was *beyond* tired!

One evening, in the winter of 1989, I chose to stay behind in my dorm room to work on some homework while a host of my dormmates decided to go play Spades. I wasn't much of a cards player, so I knew that would be a waste of my time *AND* my partner's! I couldn't call any "possible books" to save my life. Playing Spades or any other card game (except for UNO) just wasn't my thing. So, there I was; left behind, working on some Accounting homework. Accounting wasn't for me either, so I had to take frequent breaks while trying to work through it. During one of those mental breaks, I walked two doors down to visit with another dormmate who also stayed behind. We shared a thought or two and exchanged a laugh before I trekked back to my room. As I was entering my room, I saw four girls walking down that long hallway towards me. I couldn't see them clearly, but it was apparent they were headed to see me. They were walking with a vengeance. Being the curious person that I was, I stalled to see if they wanted me. *Not* to my surprise, they did. So, I invited all four of them into my room. NOT SMART! Remember, my roommate was gone, too.

The girls came in, settled themselves on my roommate's bed, and proceeded to tell me what "problems" they had with me. Those "problems" are what brought them to my room that night. I sat there in sheer dismay and disbelief as they each shared their stories about *me* with *me*. It was clear none of them liked me and had every intention on showing me just how much they didn't. After sitting there listening to them talk about a bunch of nothing, one of them (the 'Ring Leader') approached me in a physical manner. That first push led to my falling and then the other girls joined in. I remember being pushed, kicked in the stomach, having my hair pulled tightly, and smacked around…repeatedly. It all lasted approximately 10 minutes—from the time they entered my room until they scurried out from fear of being accused of the assault they'd just committed. As my luck would have it, *NO ONE* witnessed a thing! The one dormmate who was in her room didn't see anything, but she surely heard all the commotion and knew that I was struggling. When she came and knocked on my door to check on me, all the scuffle stopped. Those four girls practically ran out. To this day, I'm not sure why they wanted to hurt me. Besides the scar of my left jawline, there were no other visible signs of my attack. I was emotionally scarred.

That whole altercation humbled and changed me in so many ways. Not only do I wear that scar today; I remember the whole incident as if it happened **today**. That was yet another event that gave life to my lack of self-confidence, self-worth, and self-esteem. I truly felt like a rape victim.

That next year, I met a young man who was also a student chasing his dream of earning a college degree and making a better life for himself. We went on our first date that summer and things began to progress rather quickly from there. We soon became inseparable. There I was, enjoying the company of this young man, yet had not resolved the hurt feelings I endured from the attack just a year earlier. After two court mediations and the idea of transferring to a different college, I was *still* dealing with the hurtful feelings from the physical abuse I endured. I was not ready for a serious relationship—with anyone—yet, there I was, falling into something I wasn't ready for.

After years of being on and off, up and down, right and left, the physical abuse reared its ugly head again…and I allowed it.

From years of insecurities, immaturity, and lack of trust, the fights between us immersed and turned our union into a toxic relationship. I had sleepless nights and raging emotions of helplessness. I was losing control of who and how I was. After that relationship, I found myself in two subsequent relationships that were even more toxic and physically abusive. When would I become tired enough to end this cycle?

Eraina Tinnin

I Wish I'd Known

I wish I'd known that it's better to just walk away from such toxicity. At the tender and irresponsible age of 20, I didn't know how to do that. I was always more concerned about the other person's feelings and not so much my own. My creed was to spare their feelings, even if it means sacrificing my own. I was too dumb and naïve to know that lifestyle wasn't serving me well at all. After the last black eye, gun to my head, and being dragged on carpet and suffering third degree burns on my knee, *I got smart!* My life was worth more than that. I was worthy of being loved unconditionally and without anyone putting their hands on me. I had to learn to love myself with every flaw I possessed. I had to do a lot of self-talk to remind myself of how smart, beautiful, and deserving I was.

Words of Inspiration

When no one else shows you that unconditional love, I encourage you to do it for yourself. Don't wait for others to validate or approve of you. You **ARE** good enough just as you are.

Young girls can often get mixed up with controlling and manipulative guys, and that's where it starts. A clever, calculating guy knows how to woo a young girl, especially if she lacks self-confidence. That's when that unconquerable self-love **must** kick in. A person who's trying to control your every sense of being is NOT for you. Pay attention to those red flags that I obviously missed or was too oblivious to see.

LOVE yourself and **TEACH** others how to love you!

Eraina Tinnin

Marchella Blount is a woman with a tremendous heart for God and His people. She is a devoted wife, mother, daughter, sister, and dear friend to many. She finds these roles to be greatly rewarding.

Marchella is a passionate Playwright and finds joy and comfort in acting out the heart of God. She does not miss an opportunity to share the goodness of God and all that He has done through and for her. Her greatest desire is to utilize the gifts bestowed upon her to reach the masses and compel them to follow Christ.

Marchella attends John Wesley United Methodist Church.

Reflections: I Wish I'd Known

Daddy's Girl
By Marchella Blount

"But if the unbeliever departs, let him depart; a brother or sister is not under bondage in such cases. But God has called us to peace, for how do you know O wife, whether you will save your husband? Or how do you know, O man, whether you will save your wife? But as God has distributed to each one, as the Lord has called each one so let them walk."

(1 Corinthians 7:15-17, NKJV)

Eraina Tinnin

My Story

Sitting back thinking about the time when I was a little girl, I was so happy knowing I had a mother and father who really loved one another. My father and mother would never argue in front of my brothers and me. My father was more laid back, which allowed us to get what we wanted. My mother, on the other hand, was stricter about what we did. Every time my brothers would get in trouble, she would put them on punishment; however, my dad would say, *"Go outside"*. My father felt like boys belong outside and not on the inside. I never got in trouble and always stayed in my room, distanced from everyone. I could go outside all the time if I wanted to; however, I did not like going outside, nor did I like getting dirty. I guess I am still that way now…and I'm grown!

I never knew the day would come when my mom and dad would split up. My brothers and I were so disappointed and sad because we knew at the time, they belonged together. Well, as children, you really don't know much. I just knew at the time there was no arguing going on (they must have kept their fighting and arguing quiet). Being a child at that time, I felt a piece of life was pulling me in all types of directions. I had no way of figuring out what I should be doing. I did know that staying with my mom is what I wanted to do. I don't know why, but I just felt it was right. My father would call us and come by to see us from time to time. It was different not living together as a family. No more waking up to *"Good morning, mommy **and** daddy!"*; only *"Good morning, mommy!"*

What people don't understand when parents divorce is that they are divorcing the children as well. Usually, the one that is absent from the home is the one you don't see much. My father was in the military, so he worked a lot. I used to say to myself, *"He divorced my mom…not **us**."* He paid special attention to my youngest brother. My father used to take him fishing all the time. My brother is just like my dad. When I say 'carpenter', they can build anything. There is nothing like a father and son. However, there is nothing like a father and daughter either. I have always been close to my father. I never knew how much I wanted my father back home with us, especially with my mom.

Men don't understand this, but a girl needs a father in her life or another man will try to fill that fatherly role. Young girls without a father feel abandoned and tend to pick the wrong type of men as they get older. They look for love in all the wrong places because they are not getting the foundation a father—a man who is supposed to protect and show them how a man is supposed to treat her. Every child is affected by this in so many ways. Girls are left feeling like they are getting the right type of love because they are not being taught how to love, so they embrace "wrong" love.

Don't get me wrong: My father was there for me and I spoke to him often. Still, my parents moved on with dating other people. I knew no matter how much I prayed, I would never see them together again. I realized some things are just not meant to be, and I was okay with understanding people move on…that was until one day, I was listening to this song by Luther Vandross called *Dance with My Father*. When I heard that song, I started crying so hard. The words in that song are what I wanted to see my parents do just one last time. My mother and father would dance all the time and have so much fun. Having that picture in my mind made me so sad. I felt like Luther wrote that song just for me.

This very day, I still get sad when I hear that song. My dad is happily remarried and has moved on with his life. My mother is happy as well. My mother never remarried, but we are all happy for my father. I have a strong relationship with him as an adult because I could release to him my feelings. He said he never knew I felt that way. We cried together and don't talk about it anymore.

I do remember there was a time in my life when I reached out to God more and started reading my Bible. I would turn to Him and this verse would be right there providing comfort: *"Your father, your mother, your sister, your brother will deceive you, but the Lord will never deceive you"* (Psalm 27:10, NKJV). I felt comforted. It allowed me to go to my father and forgive him for not fighting for his marriage and his children.

I Wish I'd Known

I wish I had known I would get married and do the same thing; leave my husband without realizing the damage it may cause my children, especially my daughter. The cycle has its way of circling back around. My daughter is strong (much like myself); however, the one thing we can't do is lie to our children about anything, especially things that are out of our control. For a while, I could not tell my daughter why I left her father, and she was too young to understand what was going on. I knew as she got older, I could sit her down and talk to her about life and how we must be careful with the choices we make in life—in particular the type of men we choose. People will show you one side of them for years then, as soon as you get them in a comfortable environment, they change. Life is full of changes. I don't want my daughter to feel like she can't have a relationship with her father just because we are no longer together.

A mother should never beg a father to love his child or beg him to visit. A child should never feel alone in this world just because their parents did not make it. A child still needs hope, love, and support with everything he or she does. My daughter could not understand why her father and I split apart. She wanted answers at an early age, and I could not give them to her because I did not believe she was ready for the truth. Taking my daughter to church, having her around family, and giving her the love I knew did not fill the void—that missing piece...her father. One thing I did tell her was this:

"There will be no depression. The Lord is your Heavenly Father, and He will never leave you nor forsake you". My daughter replied, *"Yes, I know; but it is hard having your father in your life since day one and then he is gone."* I began to talk to my daughter about my experience when her grandparents split up. She then began to see the light. When she got older and could deal with things better, I told her the truth about why her father and I split up. I don't talk bad about her father, either. I always tell her wonderful things about him because no matter what, I can't judge him; only God can. My daughter is building the relationship.

Words of Inspiration

The best way to help girls is to get more involved with them at an early age. You must talk to girls because we are already emotional. For those without fathers in their lives, that makes things all the more difficult. Girls need to feel the love from both parents; however, some children may have only one parent. The loss of an absent parent is already a tragedy, and to not have one at all makes it even worse to deal with.

Learn to write in a journal all your thoughts and give it to God. Have a relationship with the Lord so He can direct your path. No, it is not easy when you can't physically see the person; however, writing is healing and will allow you to express how you feel about the situation. The Lord is the only one who can heal your heart. Everything takes time. Stay around positive people.

"Trust in the Lord with all your heart and lean not on your own understanding."

(Proverbs 3:5, KJV)

Eraina Tinnin

Nakia P. Evans, The Authentic Living Strategist, is the Founder/CEO of Authentically You Magazine. She is also the Owner and Radio Personality of Ruach Life Radio Network.

After dealing with many struggles in her life, Nakia knows what it feels like to be masked, covered, hidden, and abandoned. It is her passion and vision to help empower women to embrace who they are in Christ. She is the visionary of the Best-Selling Series, *The Woman Behind the Mask*. She wants to empower others on identifying who they are in Christ and how to remove their masks.

Facebook: Nakia P. Evans

Twitter & Instagram: @nakiapevans

Reflections: I Wish I'd Known

The Wounds Behind My Mask
By Nakia P. Evans

"For I know the plans I have for you", declares the Lord; "Plans to prosper you and not to harm you, plans to give you hope and a future."

(Jeremiah 29:11, NIV)

Eraina Tinnin

My Story

I remember laying in my bed, fearful to go to sleep because of what may happen next. I was seven years old, and the sound of footsteps approaching my room scared me like never before. I remember looking into the face of the person who was supposed to love me, protect me, and be there for me. Yet, instead of those things, I was humiliated and embarrassed of who I was. What did I do to make him do this to me? Was something wrong with me? Why must I endure this pain? This fear? I asked myself those questions for years.

You see, it wasn't just touches. It was the force of the kisses…things that, at that time, no seven-year-old should know about. I was confused. I was hurt. I was broken. What I desired was to be loved. Instead, I was broken. I wish I could say that the abuse only lasted that day, but it didn't. It lasted until I was 15 years old.

From that first touch, my life was forever changed. I began to become mean and then shut down. Of course, I learned how to mask myself when at school because I didn't want others to know what I endured—not just once, but basically every single night. My self-esteem dropped lower than anyone could possibly imagine. There was no way that I was special or that the GOD I heard of in church was so loving of me. How could HE?

Reflections: I Wish I'd Known

I grew up in church as a PK (Preacher's Kid). I had no choice. Church was something that we did all the time. Even when in church, my heart became hard. I became angry at the GOD I heard others sing about and pray to. Where was HE when I was being touched? Where was HE when I was being forced to do things? Where was HE when I was crying and scared? I heard what others were saying about GOD. I saw how much they said they loved HIM; yet, I was so angry and couldn't understand why I felt so alone and why no one was there to rescue me. I mean, He was GOD after all, right? I guess I expected some type of rescue or miracle on my behalf.

By the time I got into my teenage years, I had become a completely different person. The way I dressed changed. My attitude changed. I made it my business to hurt others because I was hurt. I pushed everyone away and wouldn't let anyone get too close to me. I wanted others to hurt just as much as I was hurting, so I used my words to try to tear others down. I also found myself turning to alcohol to dull the effects of my issues.

The summer before my 9th grade year, a situation occurred when my abuser asked me for my forgiveness. I remember sitting in the car in front of the hospital while my mom ran to get help. I was looking at him with so much hatred in my heart. How dare he ask for my forgiveness after all he had taken me through—after all he had done to me! It didn't matter to me that he was sick. It didn't matter to me that he was at the hospital. The hatred I had in my heart wouldn't allow me to forgive him. I didn't want to forgive. Sadly, that was the last time I saw him. He died a week later. I don't recall shedding one tear or feeling some type of way about his passing. At the time, I felt **FREEDOM**. I was FREE to sleep at night and not be scared of the sound of footsteps coming towards my room. I knew I would no longer have to worry about having my body used to satisfy his needs or wants.

I'll never forget one night in church… I was 19 years old and seven months pregnant. The Pastor called me to the front of the church and told me that GOD had a plan for my life. I looked at her like she was crazy! What plan could GOD possibly have for MY life? HE couldn't possibly have a plan for this girl who was damaged, broken, and now seven months pregnant out of wedlock. Even still, while I stood there looking at the Pastor like she was crazy, she repeated what she said: "GOD has a plan for your life." I tried to question that statement in every form.

How could GOD have a plan for my life after all I've done? After all I've been through? After all the questions and the dislike I had in my heart for Him at that time? How could that be possible?

Eight years later, I finally woke up to who GOD truly is and the plans HE had for my life!

I Wish I'd Known

I wish I had known before how GOD would take the very pains of my life and use it for HIS glory and HIS purpose. I was so hurt and broken during those years in my life, I didn't want to know about HIS plans...I didn't want to know what would come from those experiences.

It wasn't until I was 30 years old that I finally realized who GOD is and how HE would use my pain to bless others. At the time, I was completely masked and had lived a life of someone else for so long. I made up the person I wanted to be and would try my best to "be her", when somewhere deep inside, I knew that "she" wasn't truly the real me. The desires I had during those years were desires that others wanted of me. They were not my own. I was in a complete state of shock and having an identity crisis.

In January 2015, GOD began to take me on a journey of forgiveness. That journey wasn't easy—and it sure wasn't something I wanted to do—but I knew I had to let all of that hurt go. I had to go back to that seven-year-old girl who was sexually abused by someone whom she thought would love her. I had to forgive that man...and myself. I had to forgive family members who didn't believe me nor protect me.

It wasn't until I allowed GOD to heal me that I began to see HIS plans for my life. It wasn't until I allowed myself to forgive that

I began to open my heart up to truly be loved and to be able to love others. If I would have known how my pain would eventually become my purpose, I believe I would have started much earlier and saved myself a lot of pain.

You see, the wounds behind my mask were so great, so ugly, and so embarrassing, I didn't want anyone to see. So, I continued to mask them to hide them daily. Sometimes, I had to pile on more masks to keep things hidden. I wanted to give GOD my mask, but what HE really wanted was the wounds I was trying to hide.

Words of Inspiration

Loves, never allow the hurt that you feel to keep you imprisoned in your past. Allow the love and healing of GOD to take over and remove the hurt. No matter what has happened, no matter what has taken place, GOD has a plan for your life: to give you a hope and a future. HE will use that hurt, that pain, that mistake, and that situation for HIS glory! HE will take the very thing you want to hide and show you the beauty in it.

There is a purpose for your pain. There is a reason you had to endure. It was necessary! So, don't fret. Don't give up and don't give in. Turn to your Father, who is able to do exceedingly and abundantly above ALL that you could ever think or imagine! Turn to the Healer of your soul. Turn to **The One** who gives you purpose…**The One** who loves you unconditionally…**The One** who will give you beauty for your ashes!

Let HIM heal the wounds behind your mask!

Dr. Nikki Fisher received a Business Degree in 2003. After witnessing health challenges within herself, she began to seek answers to healing. Dr. Fisher also received a Doctor of Naturopathy Certification in 2015. She is currently pursuing a degree in Chiropractic (Life University).

Despite the challenges she faces as an older student, she continues to push on to become one of the most successful holistic doctors of her time. She wants to share what she has learned about natural health with others.

Dr. Fisher resides in the Atlanta area.

Contact her at:
nikki@imaginnewellness.com
or www.facebook.com/imaginnewellness

Reflections: I Wish I'd Known

I Took My Power Back Over My Health
By Nikki Fisher

"And God said, Behold, I have give you every herb bearing seed, which is upon the face of all the earth, and every tree, in which is the fruit of a tree yielding seed; to you it shall be for meat."

(Genesis 1:29, KJV)

****

"Let us draw near with a true heart in full assurance of faith, having our hearts sprinkled from an evil conscience, and our bodies washed with pure water."

(Hebrews 10:22, KJV)

My Story

I stopped giving my power to food when I realized that food has the power and energy to kill your dreams, steal your life, and destroy your health. The less you eat, the healthier you are and the longer you live.

My wellness journey initially started with my grandparents, mainly my grandfather Fisher. From as far back as I can remember, my grandfather Fisher would always ask me, *"Have you drank your water today?"* I was always dumbfounded. I really didn't know how to answer that question. So, I would tell my grandfather the truth (at least what I thought was the truth): *"I don't like water. It's nasty and I just can't drink it."* We continued these Q & A sessions until his passing in 2003.

When my grandfather Fisher passed of cancer, it took a toll on my life. I began to look at life differently, by questioning life, people, and situations. I also began to look at the premature death of my grandmother (Fisher's wife). To make a long story short, I had too many unanswered questions. So, I set out in search for the truth in why people die of diseases and sicknesses. When I realized that my grandparents' passing was not a natural way to die, I received my first wake-up call—but without the truth. I felt that a divine being (or what we call 'intuition') was speaking to me as I asked for wisdom, knowledge, and understanding on the truths of the unanswered questions that plagued me.

I asked family members about the reasons why certain family members died and, as well, could it have been prevented. Then, in 1995, after my mother was diagnosed with Congestive Heart Failure (the same thing happened to her mother), I had my second wake-up call. I started to wonder, *"Will I also start to experience heart issues around the time they experienced them (30 – 35 years young)?"* I was told that the development of heart issues is due to genetics. So, I said to myself, *"I will **not** have what they have because I am aware that it exists and will avoid it…like the plague!"*

Little did I know…

In 2006, I received the dreaded news that I was being diagnosed with pre-hypertension. I said to myself, **"This cannot be!"** I asked the Most High, *"Why is this happening to me?"* I, of course, assumed the doctor was correct—that was until an unexpected visitor came knocking on the door to tell me the Good News of the Bible! Keep in mind: I was praying and asking when a Seventh-Day Adventist appeared at my door. During that time, I was getting so much information downloaded to me that it became overwhelming. **I SIMPLY DID NOT KNOW WHAT THE NEXT STEP WAS!**

The Seventh-Day Adventist shared a healing foods book with me, which she ended up giving to me. The book she gave me was the sample book, and I still cherish that book until this day. She was selling a collection of story books from the Bible. On that day, she specifically told me about Genesis and what the Bible says regarding nutrition and sickness. *(Thank you, Ms. Irvine! You changed my life!)*

Not knowing exactly what steps to take, I became a vegetarian in 2006. I was able to reverse my pre-hypertension diagnosis and started seeing another doctor. I chose another doctor because I didn't want her confusing who I used to be with the newfound person I am today. While being seen by the new black female doctor, she said, *"**WOW!** You have perfect blood pressure (120/80)!"* I was amazed as well! Immediately, I said, *"I stopped eating meat."* Guess what she said in reply to that?

"If everyone stops eating meat, I wouldn't have a job!"

WOW! I was astounded that she actually admitted (indirectly) that food is the cause of disease! DING! Another wake-up call!

After becoming extremely skinny and physically weak from not knowing how to eat like a vegetarian, I started eating meat again and felt an immediate sense of relief. I was desperate to not be plagued by the hereditary disease of Congestive Heart Failure and prove to myself that it was not genetic, but simply related to the choices we make.

To make a long story short, in 2008 at the age of 35, I was diagnosed with hypertension, which is High Blood Pressure. This time, there was no doubt about the diagnosis. I continued to search and search and asked The Most High, *"How do I understand your healing foods?"*

In 2011, I started watching Netflix and came across the documentaries called *Miracle: The Beautiful Truth and Forks Over*

Knives by Gerson. I was so determined to know the truth. I flew to California the next month for the next workshop hosted by Charlotte Gerson. Her workshop taught people how to heal from cancer. DING! Another wake-up call! This was the beginning of my wellness journey.

Eraina Tinnin

I Wish I'd Known

I wish I'd known how vital water consumption was to my wellness. By me being a big picture person, just telling me to drink more water was not enough. If I would have been exposed to the documentaries (such as the ones on Netflix that changed my life), then that would have been the big picture information I needed. The thing is this: You must seek out this information because there are many entities that try to keep this information and its truth away from the public.

I wish I'd known consuming 80% fruits and vegetables would have kept me well and healthier. Currently, I have adopted an 80/20 nutritional consumption lifestyle. Being able to change one's way of thinking about food consumption and nutrition will undoubtedly take time and reeducation to this mis-educational system.

I wish I'd known how important staying active is to my wellness. For some, waking up to the causes of health challenges we face may be too late or not completely understood until their weight is considerably out of control. After being able to look at the big picture and what it has proven to show about having a sedentary lifestyle, I am here to tell you that we must wake up and take a more active approach to wellness.

I wish I'd known that gluten contributes to weight gain.

Reflections: I Wish I'd Known

I wish I'd known that all water is not created equal. The truth is in the shape of the molecules.

I wish I'd known that the molecule fructose is a poison that causes hypertension, diabetes, and heart disease.

I wish I'd known that green leafy vegetables have the power to heal your body.

I wish I'd known that sports drinks are high in fructose and salt.

I wish I'd known a high carb diet is a high fat diet.

I wish I'd known that exercise improves skeletal muscle insulin sensitivity.

I wish I'd known that fiber is a vital nutrient and should be consumed with carbs.

I wish I'd known that we should not be consuming animals' milk.

These are just a few of the knowledge-nuggets that were provided to me so that I could live a more prosperous life and fulfill the Father's purpose for my life. Now I know! I shall be free and share the knowledge of the wisdom I received with others, simply for the asking.

Words of Inspiration

I challenge you to do your research and seek nothing but TRUTH. Begin to reeducate yourself about the importance of food consumption. If one does not completely understand the science of food, it is easy to be misled. I hope what I have shared with you inspires you to live your full destiny like it did mine. You shall be an overcomer! Ask HIM and receive!

#BeEmpowered #ChooseWell #SeekTruth

"My people are destroyed for lack of knowledge: because thou hast rejected knowledge, I will also reject thee, that thou shalt be no priest to me: seeing thou hast forgotten the law of thy God, I will also forget thy children."

(Hosea 4:6, KJV)

Renee Littles is a graduate of the University of North Carolina of Charlotte with a B.A. in Organizational Communication. She is also the creator of a Christian blog, adifferentkindofnom.com, geared to encourage people on this journey called life.

Eraina Tinnin

Beautifully and Wonderfully Made
By Renee Littles

"Lord my God, I called to you for help and you healed me."

(Psalm 30:2, NIV)

My Story

I spent many years in a dark place—a dark place created by unhealthy healing techniques. Essentially, I created a prison within myself. For a long time, I built walls around me until I started to feel trapped. The walls I built high and deep to keep others out became a place even I couldn't get out of. Instead of dealing with the situations of my past, I tried to hide them by burying them. With anything and everything, I tried my hardest to forget. I thought pretending like it never happened was the answer. I was trapped within these walls with depression, low self-esteem, a feeling of worthlessness, and suicidal tendencies. Death always seemed like the path to take.

At the age of 12 and then again in high school, I attempted to kill myself. I was very withdrawn and stayed to myself. I was empty with an exterior that wouldn't allow me to be vulnerable enough to admit I needed help. To me, vulnerability was a sign of weakness. It reminded me of my childhood experiences. I blamed myself for the things that happened to me as a kid. *What if I could have done 'this'? I should have fought back. If I wasn't so weak, maybe that would not have happened to me.*

The idea of uncovering my hurts and wounds seemed impossible and uncomfortable. The truth is I had become comfortably uncomfortable with my negative baggage. But God! He never wants to leave you in a bad place. He began to tap on my heart. I could feel

Him in my spirit telling me to let go. He wanted me to give Him my past hurts and heal me the right way. The things I was seeking to feel better were not working anymore. After running for so long with the same outcome, I finally stopped. Someone once said the definition of insanity is trying to do the same thing over and over again, expecting a different result. I finally arrived at a place where I had run out of pseudo-healing methods. God was the answer! He was the answer to all my problems. Healing meant being honest with myself about where I had been. I had to allow myself to be open with God. I had to let God peel back the layers, break down the walls, and do what He does best: Pick me up and dust me off. I had to go back so that I could move forward

    I was an outgoing kid. I was outspoken, confident, and always leading my cousin around. When I was five years old, my father married his second wife. In the beginning, it was exciting! I didn't know my biological mother, and here was this seemingly nice woman telling me I could call her "mom". It started off great! She was all a motherless kid could desire in a mother. She was a woman of influence. To the outside, we were a perfect family. I was in private school. I had all the latest toys. My room was pink with beautiful white furniture. We went on family trips and outings. I would draw pictures for her. She took me to work one day, and I saw all my art hanging up. It seemed perfect! I felt comfortable. As I got older, I realized I continued that pattern…a pattern of creating a vision of perfection on the outside, even though the inside was a mess.

Reflections: I Wish I'd Known

Down the road, the dynamics of a happy mother-daughter relationship changed for the worse. Around the age of seven, the woman I saw as my mother became a vision of fear. She verbally and physically abused me. Words like, "You won't amount to anything—just like your mother!", lingered into my late 20s. I felt like I couldn't do anything right as a kid because everything I did seemed to be a trigger for her rage.

During the five years under her terrorist reign, she would beat me, tie me to poles, and leave me sitting on the cold concrete of the dark basement for hours and hours (I didn't get over my phobia of sleeping in the dark until I was 29 years old). I was no longer an outspoken, confident kid. I was empty. In the 4th grade, I learned the New York City bus transit route so that I could get to school each day. I would often daydream about what was after my bus stop. I wanted to skip my stop and go further into Queens because surely, anywhere was better than my current living situation. I was scared to go home AND scared to skip my bus stop. I felt like I was drowning in fear.

When I got older, I finally told my grandmother what happened to me. She asked me why I didn't tell my father. At that time, my father was commuting two hours to upstate New York to his job, so the only time I saw him was briefly during the week and on the weekend. Plus, "mom" threatened me by saying if I ever told anyone what she was doing, she would kill me and hide my body so that no one would ever find me. I was scared. I spent a lot of time trying to be perfect to avoid her wrath. I was always on edge.

I remember one time, I forgot an article of clothing in her mother's car. That turned into a night of hunger. I spent many nights hungry for seemingly no good reason. I was always apologizing, even if I didn't do anything wrong, because I thought it would save me from a punch or kick to the stomach. I always thought of ways to make her like me. What could I do better? I spent years striving for an unrealistic goal of perfection, afraid to mess up and scared I would do the wrong thing. I was scared to live life. I thought people saw me through her lenses.

The enemy's plan is to kill, steal, and destroy. Oftentimes, he will use people to facilitate his plan. So, for me, forgiveness was a huge part of this journey. I had already forgiven her. Later down the road, I realized she was dealing with some health issues (Lupus) that possibly played a role in her actions. That wasn't an excuse, but more of my way of understanding what she was going through. More importantly, I had to learn to forgive ME. It wasn't my fault. There was nothing I did to cause her to lash out at me.

I Wish I'd Known

I wish I would have known that I am beautifully and wonderfully made in God's image, no matter what "mom" said or thought about me. I am good enough. I am valuable. I was created with a purpose and destiny. Despite my circumstances, it's truly not about me. We go through things for God's glory. They are things that push us into God's perfect plan for us. My favorite scripture, Jeremiah 29:11 (NKJV), says, *"For I know the plans I have for you," declared the Lord. "Plans to prosper you and not to harm you, plans to give you hope and a future."* I see the things I went through as a testimony for someone else. We go through things to go back and help others in similar situations and to encourage them. I wish I would have known that you will go through processes in life to build your character. God is still peeling back layers and healing things I have tucked away so that I can become the best version of me. It's a process that happens little by little. I wish I would have known that I did not have to accept and carry around the negative things "mom" spoke into my life. I wish I would have known I had the power to speak positivity over my life.

Words of Inspiration

The journey hasn't been easy, but with God and His Word, we can stand strong and know that God has us in the palm of His hand. He didn't bring us this far to leave us hanging. The enemy's tactics are designed to destroy us and to prevent us from reaching our purpose and destiny. He wants to break us down. He wants us to feel invaluable. We must realize the enemy is already defeated! He was defeated when Jesus hung on the cross. You will overcome, rise up, and become what God has destined and purposed you to be. Sometimes, it's hard to understand God's plan—especially when suffering is involved. Still, it's all a part of His perfect plan for you. I pray you begin to see yourself through the lenses of God. We are not our depression or low self-esteem. Don't stay comfortable in negativity. You are victorious in HIM! Lean on the Lord in your situations. Allow him to heal you and make you whole. Surrender! Be Free!

Sima Clark Torian, Founder of *Butterfly Moments with Sima, LLC.,* is a Certified Life and Relationship Coach, a Singles' Strategist, an Author, and Motivational Speaker. Her life's purpose is to equip women with the life skills to cultivate healthy relationships with themselves, as well as with others by focusing on building a positive self-image.

Sima brings together a degree in Psychology, a Coaching Certification, and a harvest of painful yet purposeful life experiences, with the intention of changing the world—woman by woman.

Sima currently resides in Kernersville, North Carolina with her two handsome boys, Jeremiah and Jacoby.

Eraina Tinnin

After the Pressing...The Oil Comes
By Sima Clark Torian

"Consider it a gift, friends, when tests and challenges come at you from all sides. You know that under pressure, your faith-life is forced into the open and shows its true colors. So don't try to get out of anything prematurely. Let it do its work so that you become mature and well-developed, not deficient in any way."

(James 1:2-4, MSG)

Reflections: I Wish I'd Known

My Story

I was ready. I was so excited, I could not stand myself! It wasn't my first concert, but it was the one I most wanted to be at. I mean…the headliner was Guy! I couldn't wait to hear "Groove Me", "Piece of My Love", and "Teddy's Jam". Now, **that** was my *JAM*! We had anticipated this day for months. We were becoming adults! Our parents had agreed to allow us to drive ourselves and everything! I even purchased a new outfit for the occasion.

The lights came up for intermission. It was almost time for Guy to hit the stage. You could hear the chatter building in anticipation. This was it: The moment we had all been waiting for! Out of nowhere, as I scanned the Greensboro Coliseum, I noticed two familiar faces. It startled me. There stood a really good friend of my mother and Tony (my boyfriend at the time). They summoned us to come down from our seats. Where are we? Is this really happening? As many of our hometown friends looked on, we retrieved our things and slowly obliged, while our faces looked puzzled and confused. We were all wondering what was going on. Tony took me by the hand and escorted me out of the Coliseum while I was still asking, *"Why are we leaving?"* When we reached the concession area, I noticed that my sister had lost all of her composure in anguish. We had gained plenty of onlookers. Tony finally whispered to me that my father—my daddy—was dead.

What? Who? When? Why? Where?

I had so many questions. I could not cry yet. I needed some answers. Tony assured me it was not a dream. It was real. All I could think was, *"Not again God! Not again!"*

You see, we had just buried my dear mother two months prior. We were still grieving from the loss of the only parent we had come to know. My dad was pretty much absent in our upbringing, and mom had raised us mostly alone. After she passed, we began to build a relationship with our dad. He had just given us his blessings and told us to have a great time at the concert! When we left for the concert several hours earlier, he was standing in the front yard washing his Cadillac Seville. How could this be? My sister and I had become wards of the state (a fancy word for 'orphan') just like that. In the blink of an eye, we had become two ladies—ages 17 and 19—with no parents. Who would help us transition into adulthood? Who was going to walk me down the aisle? Who was going to help me transition into motherhood when I had my first baby? Who? God, you have some explaining to do, and I mean right NOW!

Over the course of the next week, with the help of our family, my baby sister and I planned memorial services for my dad. We had just done this not too long ago, yet there we were again. The military was gracious and was with us every step of the way. Soon after, it was time for real life to begin. Tameeka and I grew up fast…I mean really, REALLY fast! Soon after that, we were suddenly alone often, left to figure out many things we previously did not have to worry about.

Reflections: I Wish I'd Known

How was the rent going to be paid? How was college going to be paid? Where were we going to live? Do we need to get jobs?

Tameeka had not planned for life after high school, but thanks to our family and friends, we were able to get her into a college close by at the very last minute. I went back to college at the University of Virginia to try to finish out my freshman year. Tameeka stayed back and finished the final months of her senior year in high school. We had no supervision and no parental direction. We were simply surviving. My mother taught us how to survive, that was for sure! She never said a word about it, but we watched her do it day in and day out. We watched her get weary in her well-doing, but she persevered. When she got sick, her body was tired and worn. She fought as long as she could until she gave up the fight one day. The cancer had taken over her liver. There was nothing more the doctors could do for my dear mother. The night she died, my father was right by her side. They are both gone now, but the memories we have (even in its dysfunction at times) are glorious. We miss them dearly.

Since the ages of 17 and 19, my sister and I have been completely on our own. We have felt abandoned at times by many, rejected by many, thrown away by many, abused by many (physically, emotionally, mentally, and financially), and taken advantage of by many. Life has not been easy by any stretch of the imagination. Without direction, we made a lot of mistakes—and I mean a LOT of them. We have chosen all the wrong mates, desperately seeking value that we never received from our father. Trust me: There have been a lot of "what ifs" and "how comes". I have questioned God's plan for my life on occasion because life has been so hard. I have even contemplated taking my life a few times because life had gotten so tough to bear. Why, God? Why so much pain?

Then, one day…one fine day…it all made sense! When I turned 40, I began to pray and ask God to make sense of it all. Surely, all this pain could not be in vain. Surely! In my prayer time, God promised that He would use it all…every single drop. The rejection. The abandonment. The abuse. The disappointment. All of it! He asked me if I truly believed Romans 8:28. I have quoted that passage of scripture many times, but it wasn't until then that I truly believed it. There would be double for my shame and beauty for my ashes. I knew with confidence that I loved God, but I wasn't sure about being called to His purpose. I prayed more…and then some more. Then, God spoke! He gave me a mandate to help women overcome pain, to smack that devil in the head and let him know that no pain would be in vain, and that God would use every bit. *(You may insert a **HALLELUJAH** right there!)* Finally, I had purpose! I was here for a purpose. I am still here for a purpose. This level of clarity is mind-boggling. It is almost like putting in the last piece of the puzzle and stepping back to look at what you have created. God wants to use ME!

From there, I began to look at every struggle, even down to losing both parents, as "necessary". I know that sounds crazy. I know you are wondering, "Who in their right mind thinks like that?" Well, it was necessary for God's perfect will for my life. As much as I love and miss my parents, it was not in God's plan for my life to have them here except for the time that I had them. This is a hard philosophy to absorb, I am sure; however, I believe God knew that I would not fully understand this level of revelation until I was 40 years old.

God is such a gracious Father and knows all of His children well, including you. He knows everything about you; your insecurities, your pains, your desires, as well as your failures. He orchestrates your life based on how He, in His infinite wisdom, believes you will be successful—even down to the timing of it all. 3 John 1:2 says, *"Beloved, I wish above all things that you prosper and be in health"*. Our Father's ultimate desire for each of us is to prosper. He wants this for all of us!

So, now, at the age of 47, I spend my days encouraging other women to stay the course and fight for their peace each and every day. God promised to use everything that you've endured to create a beautiful story so that He can get all the glory and, above all things, that you would prosper because of it.

Eraina Tinnin

I Wish I'd Known

I wish I'd known that God takes care of His own every time. He never fails. He can do all things but fail. He is faithful to complete everything that He starts. EVERYTHING! I wish I had learned to trust His plan much earlier in life. This would have decreased the time I wasted worrying about things that He took care of anyway. I wish I could get that time and, most of all, that peace back.

Words of Inspiration

As long as we are breathing, bad things will happen. It is just the reality of being human. I want to encourage you: When these things happen, try not to focus on the "why" as much as the "what". Instead of asking God, *"Why did you allow this?"* or *"Why did they do this to me?"*, after you have processed it all, ask God, **"What would you have me do with this?"** He will answer. Expect it. If we never have a problem, we will never know that God will be able to fix it. He always does everything with purpose. All things! So, next time, take a moment, laugh, and say, *"God, I cannot **WAIT** to see what you are going to do with this one!"*

After the pressing...the oil comes!

Praise God for the oil! Grace & Peace!

Stacey R. Simmons, a native New Yorker, is called into the kingdom for such a time as this. She has obtained three degrees: a Bachelors in Information Science, a Masters of Business Administration in Organizational Leadership, and a Master of Arts in Pastoral Counseling. She is a general member of Alpha Kappa Alpha Sorority Incorporated.

Stacey is the wife of Pastor Ian T. Simmons. Together, they serve in ministry at The Ambassador Pentecostal Church in Christ, Bronx, New York.

Stacey's life is led by the scripture found in Hebrews 11:1: *"Now faith is the substance of things hoped for, the evidence of things not seen"*.

Eraina Tinnin

Abandoned But Not Alone
By Stacey Simmons

"Even if my father and mother abandon me, the Lord will hold me close."

(Psalms 27:10, NLT)

My Story

It can be difficult to walk in who God has called you to be when you were never affirmed by the man who was supposed to love you first here on earth. I grew up without my father being around. My parents were married three years before they conceived me; however, they were divorced by the time I was a year old. All I can remember is my father never being around. I would speak to him on birthdays and Christmas. When he would call, he would give me his cell phone number and tell me that I can call him whenever I wanted to hear from him. I would take him up on his offer from time to time, but when I called, the telephone number would be disconnected. I would have to wait for the next "special occasion" to hear from him to be told he got a new number. The only time my father would show up publicly to support me was graduations. When he came, I always felt as if he was embarrassing me. To everyone on the outside, we were the perfect separated family. To me, it was all one big lie.

My family and friends used to make fun of me and call me names because I wore glasses and my mother would put beads in my hair. They would call me "Stacey Beads", for it matched my hair and rhymed with my maiden name. To them, they thought it was a cute nickname for me. To me, it was so annoying. Despite the lack of my father's presence in my life and the names I was repeatedly called, I rose above the statistics. I've always received acknowledgements throughout my time in school. I was successful and well-accomplished to others. Deep inside, I still felt like I was a nobody. At the end of the day, I longed to have my father in my life. I wanted my father to tell me that I'm beautiful. I wanted him to validate me and tell me that he loved me. I wanted to be confident in knowing that if I could count on anyone, I could always count on my father. However, that was not the cards of life I was dealt.

Not having a father in my life caused me to jump in and out of relationships throughout my late teens into my early twenties. I put myself in harm's way multiple times by dating boys/men who were members of gangs. Back then, I thought putting my life on the line was 'cute'—knowing that gang members who knew my boyfriend at the time would mean protection. In all actuality, it wasn't safe…nor was it smart. In my 20s, I started approaching the people in my life with a *"What's in it for me?"* mentality, especially when it came to men. I started playing their games and soon, it got to the point where I started playing the games better than them! If I felt that they were catching feelings for me, I would back out to avoid commitment. I restricted myself to only having relationships based on meeting my temporary emotional and physical needs at that time.

Those unhealthy relationships throughout my late teens into adulthood caused me to harm myself by attempting to cut my wrists, suicidal thoughts, depression, and extreme weight loss. I had a lack of trust in people and lack of confidence in myself. I even lost faith in God. It wasn't until I reached the age of 25 that I started to really do some soul-searching to find out who I was, why I did the things I did, and how, if I made God a priority, my life would be all the better for it.

Due to the continuous healing that has taken place in my life over the course of time, I was able to welcome my father back into my life. I can love and respect him now, despite how our father-daughter relationship originally started. It doesn't mean that I forget, but I do forgive him for his lack of presence in my life. As a result of my father not being present in my younger years, I was able to discover my Heavenly Father on a closer level. In return, He gave me a husband who loves me unconditionally, despite my flaws and my unfortunate past.

Eraina Tinnin

I Wish I'd Known

I didn't need people, things, and temporary satisfaction to make me feel whole. All I needed was to know God for myself and solidify my relationship with Him.

When people tell you to not have sex before marriage, they are telling you the truth. Sex before marriage can cause a lot of emotional and mental disturbances later in life.

Me not having a father while growing up was and is still not uncommon. There are many children today who are growing up in a single-parent household, primarily without a father.

Words of Inspiration

You are beautiful, regardless of whether you hear it from those closest to you or not. Tell yourself in the mirror every day that you are beautiful. Do what you need to do in a positive way to align yourself with this known fact because IT IS TRUE!

Just because you may have been raised without your father doesn't mean you are not important. God is the Father of all fathers, and He will be there to carry you through every step of the way.

Don't be ashamed to tell your story. It can have positive effects on others. You can free your family and friends and, as a result, generational curses can be broken.

Sometimes, our circumstances are what draw us closer to God. The truth be told, if trials and tribulations did not disturb our lives, how would we know who God is and what He is capable of doing?

Tameeka Clark-McClain is an Operational Manager for Kroger for 24 years. She received the Progressive Grocer Top 100 Women of the Year Award in 2008. Her pioneering work in retail demonstrates her motivation to embrace people's wholeness.

Tameeka holds a Bachelor's Degree in Business Administration from Winston Salem State University. She is also Co-Founder of Fabulous4Tees bling t-shirts. Tameeka is a first-time author, sharing her story in hopes to persuade young ladies from making unfavorable choices and listening to the whispers of God.

Tameeka is a single mother of one daughter, Londyn, to whom she is well-dedicated to in Roanoke, Virginia.

Reflections: I Wish I'd Known

The Invisible Fire
By Tameeka Clark-McClain

"Seek His will in all you do, and He will direct your paths. Don't be impressed with your own wisdom. Instead, fear the Lord and turn your back on evil. Then, you will gain renewed health and vitality."

(Proverbs 3:6-7, NLT)

Eraina Tinnin

My Story

That moment, I was in the hotel room…shivering like I had flu-like symptoms. I spent many nights on the road from city to city, hoping to get back home to my deacon (at least that's what I thought). My mind was focused on the days to come as the dream of a lifetime was quickly approaching. My time was running out. What was I going to do with so much on my plate and no one to help me get through the day that I thought was going to be the best day ever? I looked to the hills where my strength comes from. I kept looking and praying for the strength I needed. I had a few more days to get the last few touches for the ceremony complete. I prayed, *"Lord, help me get through this process, as I only have me to do this because no one has my back"*. I knew that no one believed what I was doing was good for me…except me. I was feeling so in love with that fact of living the dream that all beautiful queens look forward to.

I only had one more time to practice the song I was going to sing to him as I walked down the aisle. My pianist was nervous and coaching me at the same time. I was trying to surprise him, so he was unaware of my presence with the pianist. My nerves took over my body, my voice, and everything about me.

I looked at my pianist and said, *"I can't do this."*

He replied, *"Yes, you can. God has never failed you yet! Just have faith and keep singing."*

Reflections: I Wish I'd Known

I Believe in You by Whitney Houston became a new version called *I Believe in You...**Not Me**...*with Tameeka's nerves taking the lead.

My heart was filled with so many thoughts of love and peace, as he was so kind and loving. We had so much in common. We laughed so much together that life would not be the same without the jokes and laughter. Upon opening my eyes every morning, I was embraced with smiles and laughs that were long-lasting forever. The most participating love we had was riding those crotch rockets (motorcycles) going 120 MPH on I-81. The thrills brought us together even more! Afterwards, he would smack my butt and say, *"That's my girl! I can't find anyone else like you, Covergirl!"*

I so believed in him, as the short time of engagement had come to an end. He chose my diamond to be a past, present, and future one-karat with the future held in the palm of his hand. It was shining (like Rihanna would say)! Not one, but three diamonds! I couldn't wait to get the two bands we picked out to make that set POP! The time is here...yes, it is HERE!

The wedding party arrived at the house for the rehearsal festivities. My vision of silver and black popping with red roses was the elegance of our beauty together. The girls and violinist arrived one-by-one. All the guys were local and sliding in one at a time. The time came for the planner to get things started. The caterer had prepared the food and the bamboo vases were displayed everywhere for the taking. The alcoholic beverages flowed through the garage. My fiancé was drinking to the point that he could not keep his hands off of me. I began to wonder, *"Why was he being so disrespectful in front of our guests?"* My mouth said, *"It's just him. He will be okay."* Well, 'just him' was exactly what it was for the entire night. One beverage led to another…and then another. I could feel all of my family and friends stalking me about the behavior that was being portrayed. It was harsh in the eyes of others. I was blinded and so much in love, nothing could stop me from accepting the overly-physical touches, boisterous voice, and pushy directions.

I vividly recall the planner saying, *"Everyone; it's time to clean up and get to the church to decorate. The guys can stay here and finish up while we get to the church."* My fiancé was so pushy that he yelled, **"Get this s**t up and let's go!"** So, just like that, everyone moved when he said 'move'. We loaded up all the necessities and headed to the house of the Lord. When we arrived at the church, there was a revival still in process. All the ladies went to the dining hall as directed, and the guys followed my fiancé. I took a peek up the stairwell to see where they guys were and there stood his coworker and church friend looking back at me from the top of the stairs. She gave me this look of turmoil and then up went her middle finger as she mouthed the words, *"F**k you."* My nerves were tore up again because this same chick had harassed and disrespected me several other times while in my man's presence.

At this point, I had yet to tell my sister or anyone else about enduring the behavior of this chick simply because I was in love. For whatever the reason, homegirl was out to sabotage me because I was going to be the new wife. I was a nervous wreck…again. This chick headed to the front of the church to have a seat. I didn't know my fiancé had moved to the front of the church and sat his happy hips in the seat directly behind her. In my mind, I thought, *"Lord, he has entered the church and sat down smelling like a liquor barrel."* My stomach did somersaults, and it was more than just nervous butterflies.

Stress and more stress was what I had written all over my face. Suddenly, I hear a bunch of commotion coming from the front of the church. Everyone was yelling, cussing, and pulling on my fiancé in an attempt to remove him from the sanctuary. I looked up and saw my sister and cousin. They were telling me what happened…

Apparently, he went into the church during the revival service and cussed that chick out. All I heard flowing through the air was **"B***h, this!" and "B***h, that!"** The pastor instructed the men to remove him from the sanctuary. The drama was pushed straight out the door. I fell to my knees on the sidewalk and cried my eyeballs out. The fire was so hot coming out of my body, I ran to the car and drove off—fully enraged! At that point, I had to reveal to everyone in the car what had just transpired.

Once I returned home, I felt so embarrassed and humiliated that I went straight to my room, fell on my queen bed, and would not move. All I remember was everyone coming into the room to check on me. All of a sudden, the Pastor enters. He entered the room and said, *"Tameeka, I cannot and will not marry you tomorrow. He just disrespected the church and me."* I felt like I was faced with death and the house both sounded and smelled like a funeral home. The wedding party was sitting around the house as if they were there for a viewing. That day became the worst day of my life…one I had never imagined. It was definitely not one I imagined would end as it did.

The next morning, the sun peeked through the curtains. When I opened my eyes, there he was lying beside me. I didn't know whether to scream, cry, or embrace him. I was a very confused young lady and couldn't see the forest for the trees. When I headed to the living room (as humble as I knew how), there sat red roses displayed all throughout the house. The catered food was set up on the kitchen counter, and the planner was fussing with the hairstylist. I became a zombie walking through the living room. It was time for everyone to leave and all of my girls were begging me, *"**Please** don't go on that honeymoon trip with him!"* That bubble in my head reminded me of all that his boys had told me: *"**Don't do it!** He will never change!"*

Two days later, we were in Aruba…honeymooning without a wedding. A year later, I was walking down the aisle just as confused as I was the night before the "first" wedding. How did this happen nine years later? I had put my whole body in that fireplace with just my head peeking out. I was trying to be saved by the whispers of God that I ignored the first time. Was I young, dumb, in love, infatuated, desperate, disobedient, or ignoring my heart?

The answer is: **All of the above.**

I Wish I'd Known

All things are laid out for you for a reason even a blind man can see. Don't fall short of acknowledging that your surroundings can be purpose blockers and your soul has to be whole to get it. Just because you feel lonely it's ok to be lonely. When you experience toxic behavior and it doesn't change, or a relationship is just too toxic, send them forward in life with compassion, and then move forward with your life even with the hurt.

Words of Inspiration

I do not believe you can have the peace of God until you are at peace with God. This peace transcends or surpasses all human understanding. This peace guards our hearts and minds. Do you have peace with God today? Find peace before you make choices that are detrimental to your life. Leaning on your own understanding can sometimes put you in the pit of fire that will cause you so much chaos in your life. Follow your heart and listen to God's whispers. If you see the writing on the wall, ask God to deliver you!

Eraina Tinnin

Telicia Volter is a wife of 18 years, mother of three, Best-Selling Author, aspiring Motivational Speaker, Licensed Minister, and Founder of Greater Is She. Telicia has a heart for women and relates to them in many areas, including self-worth and fear. Not only does she want to see women win in all areas of life, she has a desire to see this throughout the Body of Christ. Understanding the challenges of falling and getting back up again, she seeks to motivate and encourage others with authentic transparency.

Connect with Telicia at:

Facebook: Telicia Volter
Or via email at t.volter@gmail.com

Royalty in the Rubble
By Telicia Volter

"For we are His workmanship [His own master work, a work of art], created in Christ Jesus [reborn from above— spiritually transformed, renewed, ready to be used] for good works, which God prepared [for us] beforehand [taking paths which He set], so that we would walk in them [living the good life which He prearranged and made ready for us]."

(Ephesians 2:10, AMP)

Eraina Tinnin

My Story

I can't remember what triggered his rage this time. I don't recall if I said something (or nothing at all). It is hard to say. It could have been anything. It could have been nothing. I just can't recall. I do remember him swerving in and out of traffic in my car. I remember him hurling threats, promising me that he was going to teach me a lesson I will never forget. I remember trying to jump out of the car to find safety. He was determined to not allow escape. Somehow, he grabbed me and forced me to close the door. That attempt at escape just angered him more. I remember the increasingly wild look in his eyes as he searched for the perfect place to make good on his promise.

A few minutes later, he turned into a school bus barn. He drove past rows and rows of buses until we reached a narrow opening between a bus and a fence. There was just enough room for him to back the car in, out of sight from the world around us. Seclusion. He flew around to my side of the car and, in one swift motion, yanked my door open with one hand and tossed me out of the car with the other. I felt sharp jabs on my stomach and legs as I slid down the rocks near the fence. His fist connected with my skull. Then, his shoe went into my stomach. He was kicking me! I remember the shock.

This was new. He'd never done this before.

As I laid there on a pile of rocks and rubble, I remember telling myself, *"**NEVER** again! This will never happen to me again!"*

Reflections: I Wish I'd Known

Eventually, he stopped, apologized, helped me to my feet, and cried. That was nothing new; however, I was sick of it. No one deserved that treatment. I didn't deserve it, that's for sure!

How did I get here?

It started with my childhood and a great demise of my self-worth. I was well-known in the small town I grew up in. It wasn't because we had the biggest house on the block or because I was the winner of the town's yearly pageant. I wasn't a cheerleader. Neither did I belong to the popular cliques that flooded the halls of my school. I was the chubby, identical twin granddaughter of a preacher in a predominantly white town. I was the kid who didn't live with her parents. I was the kid who looked and dressed differently than everyone else. I didn't get too far in childhood before I was constantly reminded of how "different" I was.

Being different was negatively highlighted in the worst ways possible; so much so, I ended up switching to a predominantly black school. I will confirm what you are probably already thinking: No, I wasn't received well. The proper-speaking, nerdy black girl in oxfords, knee high socks, and a dress was shunned right out of the gate! I wish I could say I was one of those kids who didn't care about fitting in, but I did. I didn't want to be the fat kid, preacher's kid, nerdy kid, black kid, or the different kid. I just wanted to be a cool kid. I wanted to be the kid who didn't get teased and the one who fit in.

The day I became a cool kid was when anger and fatigue collided. That day, I was being teased on the bus before school—and

I was tired of it! A fight with significantly older girls ensued, and it spread like wildfire. I had to disregard the rules and disrespect myself and others to fit into their standard of "cool"! Isn't that something? Once I was "in", repeated acts of defiance had to continue if I wanted to STAY "in". The things that used to matter to me (like grades and attendance) were put on the backburner. The desperation of wanting to belong trumped my desire to want to do right by myself. From this desperation, I made a series of bad decisions, one after the other.

Without enlisting God's help in my rejection, I either latched on super-tight with a grip that even Samson couldn't break OR I inflicted the same rejection on others. I either did the abandoning OR made myself so unhealthily available that honoring myself became nonexistent. That was how I found myself in yet another abusive relationship at 17 years old. I had to have a relationship, just like everyone else I was hanging around. Like I mentioned, I was "in" and had to STAY "in". It has been my experience that when God is left out of the equation, there's no peace. My life was evidence of that!

I Wish I'd Known

I wish I would have known that being different is better than being devalued. I wish I'd known that if I knew and understood my worth, I wouldn't have wasted time trying to prove to people that I was worthy. I wish I'd known that my lack of self-worth would create major issues in the roles I would take on such as wife, mother, and friend. If I didn't understand how to value myself, how could I instill that in my children? I held on to people I called 'friends' and allowed myself to be devalued. These created issues in my marriage because I didn't cut them off. I wish I'd known that I didn't have to believe them. I wish I would have known that I stayed too long in the rubble.

Eraina Tinnin

Words of Inspiration

Self-worth, by definition, is the opinion you have about yourself and the value you place on yourself. It doesn't matter what they said. It doesn't matter what they still say. What does God's Word say? YOU are the head, and NOT the tail. YOU are above, and NOT beneath. YOU are made in HIS image. YOU are HIS masterpiece. Don't allow their labels to make and/or keep you stuck. There is value in God's vision of you and for your life. You don't have to believe what they say. Don't let their labels cancel out God's Word. Don't let their voices speak louder to you than God's voice. It's okay to permanently press mute on self-esteem stealers and vision-killers. Get out of that rubble! Upgrade your opinion and revive the vision. Believe the Word of God! Live the life God prearranged for you, not the 'like' they rearranged for you! You are worth it! You are the daughter of The King!

Toni Freeney is a First Time Author, Business Owner, wife, and mother of two children. Her passion is helping as many people as possible by sharing her life experiences and giving advice on how to deal with difficult situations. Spreading Love is her end goal and saving lives comes second nature to her. She loves everyone. She does her best writings when she is comfortable in disclosing truth on serious topics.

Toni is a free spirit who loves God and has crazy Faith. Her life is filled with action-packed adventures that are worth the read.

Eraina Tinnin

Putting in Work Isn't Enough
By Toni Freeney

"For as the body without the spirit is dead, so faith without works is dead also."

(James 2:26, KJV)

Reflections: I Wish I'd Known

My Story

This is a story dear to my heart because I was only 19 years old and unaware of politics, racism, and culture shock. "THE UNIVERSITY" changed my life's VIEWS. As an Israelite girl, being born in Compton, California and raised in South Central California was rough. The only security in my life was my grandmother, who died five years earlier. At that point in my young life, in need of a breakthrough after coming very close to dropping out of high school (but still managed to graduate), I desired a way out of the ghetto.

My very first experience on a college campus was when I started working at "The University" at the tender age of 16 years old. Desperate to change my situation at home, I prayed hard and got a job as a cashier at Jarl's Sr., a fast food restaurant on campus. "The University" was a world inside a world with its own credit union, restaurants, theater, church, grocery store, and post office. I quickly learned the benefits, which included free tuition for the full-time employees, their spouses, and children. This was a dream come true! Watching the foreigners use this process of working a labor job to put their families through a prestigious university was brilliant! I quickly understood how the system worked.

As soon as I turned 18 years old, I applied to become a full-time employee as a Campus Security Officer (CSO)! Although the waiting list was long and the hiring process was rigorous, I was determined to better my life by advancing to a full-time position on campus. Once hired into the Security Department at "The University", I was sure my life was set until retirement. I planned on doing my 15 years and retiring before the age of 35, all while putting my family through school. My heart and mind were set as I built my credit to excellent and became a role model for my peers. I hadn't planned on ever doing anything to ruin an opportunity where my children and spouse would get a **FREE EDUCATION.**

"The University" had given me an illusion of security that would be maliciously taken away from me because of lust, greed, and power! They say 'Pride comes before the fall". Well, I was beyond proud—surpassing my aunts and most adults around me by bringing in $40,000 annually (with overtime) in 1993. I did everything in my power by putting in the work to keep it, but that was not enough! All my dreams were snatched away by a vicious, nasty supervisor who wasn't even over me but was obsessed with me.

On March 2, 1992, I was hired as a CSO. The Rodney King riots broke out April 29th through May 4th that same year. Being an officer for only two months, I was ready to quit! We were right in the middle of the chaos. I was beyond scared but wasn't going to let anything stand in the way of my future. Terrified but prayed up, I survived the riots, racism, and even the gangs!

Nonetheless, it was the sexual harassment of "Supervisor Sike Darvey" (also known as SD) that was my demise. He would not take **"No!"** for an answer. I made him fully aware of my boyfriend; my idol and a gang member from my neighborhood. He was doing time in jail and I was dedicated to him. I was not remotely interested in SD at all. When I made that very clear, it infuriated him even more. Unaware of the fact that SD was having sex with every female coworker except me, he felt I was a trophy he had to get. Daily, sexual advances were made. It made me feel ashamed and helpless. I would pray that he would just leave me alone and let me do my job, but he insisted that I have sex with him—although he was married with children. When I would pull into the parking structure for work and see his car, I would vomit by my car before entering the building. I was stripped of my dignity and pride as a teen girl. He used his power to try and intimidate me, but I was from the streets and am a fighter. Coming to work early and sure to be on point with my assignments wasn't enough, though. SD would touch himself in front of me and ask if I liked it. After his advances were denied and reported, he stopped and turned into the supervisor from hell. He tortured me daily, which made me physically, mentally, and emotionally ill.

Unfortunately, it came down to me checking myself into MISER Private MENTAL Hospital. After losing it all and fighting about four plus years with a team of "contingency-based" attorneys (combined with a lot of prayers), I was victorious. The truth prevailed in my "sexual harassment worker's compensation" case against "The University". I won $25,000 in the first lawsuit of its kind that I had ever heard of! I was literally destroyed in my field as an officer. I felt lost and as if my life was ruined because everything I had worked for was taken away. Until this day, I feel my life would have been financially secure had this not taken place. It took everything away that I had planned and hoped for.

At times, I still digress to *"What if?"*, but I'm quickly reminded of the beautiful yet painful journey my life ended up taking. My plans were not God's plans! The Most High God—my Creator—had a much different plan for my life. I'm very grateful as I write this story 25 years later and have lived the lesson that was being taught. That is why my works were not enough. I had to dig into the faith that my grandmother instilled into me before her passing. Once I accepted the closed door that GOD shut tightly, my life was changed forever. Had I stayed on that job, I would have never traveled the world, had my children, or met my amazing husband. I realize that my Creator was yet in control of my destiny, no matter how much turbulence I experienced in my teen and young adulthood years. Sometimes we feel alone, but it's just the Creator preparing us for what is to come.

I Wish I'd Known

In hindsight, if I had known what I know today, I probably wouldn't change much about my actions; however, I would have protected my mind. Growing up fatherless was a disadvantage for me when dealing with men in my life in general. I wouldn't have stressed to the point of being hospitalized in a private mental institution for 21 days. I definitely wouldn't have spent the $25,000 lawsuit carelessly. I wish I could have recognized that my life was taking a crash course in politics, racism, and culture shock. I wish I had remained calm. It wasn't easy, but I kept putting in the work and kept my faith, which ended in my victory with the help of the Creator because I can do all things through Him. Life is a lesson. As we grow with wisdom and knowledge, we realize it's all in the plan. Now, as a mid-aged woman, my advice to anyone experiencing 'Sexual Harassment' is to STAND YOUR GROUND and document the instances of abuse. Stay prayed up and REMOVE yourself as soon as possible from that situation. Until this day, I am haunted by the thought of this situation stealing all my dreams. However, I see the handiwork of the Creator who says, "I'm in control of your future, and that wasn't in my plans. I have greater for you!" So, I'm very thankful for all my tests, as now I'm able to TESTIFY!

I pray this will encourage you to continuously fight for your rights and never give up on your dreams. Today, I am a mother of two and the owner of my own business. I didn't need to lean on "The

University" because as long as I leaned on GOD, I've always made it through the storm. Always keep your faith in the Most High Creator and you can't go wrong!

Words of Inspiration

Be encouraged to always stand for what is right and just. While going through this ordeal, it made my faith a lot stronger and made me a wiser person. If you find yourself in this situation, first seek God for guidance on how to handle it. Take proper actions and make sure you know all of your rights. As a woman of God, you will go through trials and tribulations. Weapons will form, but they won't prosper against you when you seek God. Always be encouraged knowing you are more than a conqueror through the Most High God who is your strength.

Words from the Presenter

I pray this book was a blessing to you. The co-authors are amazing, courageous women who shared very personal parts of themselves with the world. Some of their testimonies are unbelievable and may have had you in total disbelief. My desire is that the stories gave you a sense of hope. If you are going through something or if you do in the future, I pray these stories help you see that YOU CAN MAKE IT THROUGH. God doesn't put more on you than you can bear. If they made it, YOU CAN, TOO!

I would love to hear your thoughts on the book. Please connect with me at www.erainatinninunlimited.com and click on the 'Contact Me' tab.

Meet Eraina Tinnin

Eraina Tinnin, the "Inspirational Powerhouse", is an Empowerment Coach, International Best-Selling Author, and Self-Love Strategist. She has been named an "Encourager" because of her unfailing ability to lift the spirits of others.

She is Founder of Eraina Tinnin Unlimited, a contributing writer with Authentically You Magazine, Author of *Becoming a Beautiful You* and *You Are a Gift*; Co-Author of *Healing Toxic Habits, Affirmations & Antidotes That Remind Me,* and *The Woman Behind The Mask: Identifying The Woman Hidden*. She is Co-Host of The Beautiful You Authentic You Radio Show and Co-Founder of Beautiful You Authentic You.

Eraina holds a Master's Degree in Human Services with a Specialization in Marriage and Family Therapy and resides in North Carolina with her husband, Corey.

www.ingramcontent.com/pod-product-compliance
Lightning Source LLC
Chambersburg PA
CBHW071517080526
44588CB00011B/1457